# SUBWAY SERIES

## A Year of New York Baseball

By the Staff of **The New York Times**

# SUBWAY SERIES

## A Year of New York Baseball

ISBN 0-930881-02-9
Manufactured in the United States of America
First printing 2000

THE SUBWAY SERIES: A YEAR OF NEW YORK BASEBALL
    EDITOR: Nancy Lee
    TEXT EDITOR: Mike Hale
    PHOTO EDITORS: Stephen J. Jesselli, Francisco P. Bernasconi
    DESIGNER: Barbara Chilenskas of Bishop Books
        *Subway Series logo designed by:* Wayne Kamidoi
    PRODUCTION EDITOR: William P. O'Donnell

SPECIAL THANKS TO: Neil Amdur, Mitch Belitz, Laura Billingsley, Morin Bishop, Tom Carley,
Andrea Cautela, Dave Frank, Greg Hamlin, John Hammond, Jeff Honea, Stuart Lavietes,
Mike Levitas, Bert Lightbourne, Barbara Mancuso, Jim Mones, Alyse Myers, Teresa Power,
Lee K. Riffaterre, Claire Spiezio, Ken Wenthen, the Picture Desk, the Photo Lab and the
incomparable photographers of The New York Times.

THE SUBWAY SERIES: A YEAR OF NEW YORK BASEBALL was prepared by
Bishop Books, Inc.
611 Broadway
New York, New York  10012

Cover photographs—left (Mariano Rivera): CHANG W. LEE; right (Robin Ventura): CHANG W. LEE.
Half-title page (special No. 7 Subway Series train outside Shea Stadium): OZIER MUHAMMAD.
Title page (World Series Game 2 in Yankee Stadium): OZIER MUHAMMAD.
Back Cover photograph (Yankee Stadium fans): CHANG W. LEE.

10  9  8  7  6  5  4  3  2  1

# Contents

# A New York Tradition Returns

BY GEORGE VECSEY

New Yorkers do not like waiting.

It is not by accident that the phrase "New York minute" is widely understood to consist of far fewer than 60 seconds.

Given this communal impatience, it was with great frustration that New York endured 44 years between Subway Series—that is to say, a baseball World Series between two teams reachable by mass transportation in the Big City.

That inexplicable deprivation ended in the year 2000 with a Subway Series between the Yankees and the Mets. Needless to say, the long-overdue series carried anticipation of momentous games and cataclysmic events.

New Yorkers tend to think they are the center of the universe, and deserve a Subway Series every year or two. This sense of entitlement is ingrained from there having been 13 such intramural World Series from 1921 through 1956, always with the New York Yankees playing either the New York Giants or the Brooklyn Dodgers.

The rivalries among the three ancient New York teams were based on local stereotypes and home-grown feuds, which, as everyone knows, are the most dangerous, producing civil wars and other such niceties.

The New York Giants played in the Polo Grounds alongside the Harlem River in upper Manhattan. For several early decades, they were one of the lordliest teams in baseball. After a while, however, Dodger and Yankee fans would accuse Giant fans of shabby and illogical nostalgia.

The Brooklyn Dodgers—named for the practice of dodging trolleys in that borough—were generally a laughable franchise (Dem Bums being one of their nicknames), but in 1941 they began reaping pennants through their excellent farm system. Nevertheless, Yankee and Giant fans accused them of being seedy eccentrics.

The Yankees, originally from Baltimore and then lowly tenants of the Giants, did not win their first pennant until 1921, with a player named George Herman (Babe) Ruth, who was essentially stolen from the Boston Red Sox. Yankee fans saw themselves as salt-of-the-earth patrons of superior baseball. Dodger and Giant fans saw them as stuffy front-runners.

The first Subway Series took place in 1921, with the Giants thumping the Yankees. The same thing happened in 1922. But in 1923, the Yankees moved across the river to the Bronx, to the new stadium that would soon be known as The House That Ruth Built.

Ruth did not hit a home run in the first Subway Series game held in the park he had made possible. However, an inside-the-park home run was committed by the man who would become the patron saint of the Subway Series

and New York baseball in general, one Charles Dillon (Casey) Stengel, who had played in the 1916 World Series for the Dodgers, and was now a member of the Giants.

As the 33-year-old Stengel huffed and puffed his way around the bases, he was said to have stuck out his tongue at the Yankees, who had the last laugh, winning the Subway Series in six games.

The Yankees beat the Giants twice more in 1936 and 1937 with a young center fielder named Joseph Paul DiMaggio. Then they bushwhacked the Dodgers in five games in 1941. The third victory was the most memorable, with the Dodgers' catcher, Mickey Owen, let-

ting the third strike of the potential final out get past him, setting up a four-run Yankee rally.

After the war came an unparalleled decade: seven Subway Series in 10 years. The Yankees beat the Dodgers in 1947 in one of baseball's most epic Series, with the Dodgers using the first African-American player of the century, Jackie Robinson. The Dodgers had wonderful moments, like Cookie Lavagetto, a veteran pinch-hitter, breaking up a no-hit bid by Bill Bevens with two outs in the ninth to win the fourth game, and Al Gionfriddo, an obscure left fielder, robbing DiMaggio of a homer to help win the sixth game. However, the Yan-

**Venerable Yankee Stadium was the site of 11 Subway Series, including a memorable matchup between the Dodgers and Yankees in 1955 (above), before the Mets and Yankees clashed in 2000.**

kees won the Series in seven behind a relief pitcher, Joe Page.

In 1949, the Yankees beat the Dodgers in five with Tommy Henrich clubbing a homer off Don Newcombe in the bottom of the ninth to win the first game, 1–0. The new manager of the Yankees was none other than Casey Stengel, who would ultimately win 10 pennants in 12 years with the Yankees.

In 1951, old DiMaggio and young Mickey Mantle played alongside each other briefly, and the Yankees beat a weary Giants team that had just defeated the Dodgers in the classic playoff with Bobby Thomson's home run. In 1952 and 1953, the Yanks beat the Dodgers again, using a combination of stars and surprising role players.

In 1955, the Dodgers finally won, and bells pealed all over the so-called Borough of Churches. For Dodger fans, it was the shining moment of a lifetime, a reward for serial humiliations.

The last Subway Series of that era, in 1956, achieved typically extravagant New York standards, involving the first and only perfect game in the history of the World Series. Don Larsen kept 27 consecutive Dodgers from reaching first base, which led to yet another World Championship flag fluttering in the Bronx.

After the 1957 season, both the Dodgers and Giants left town for a western state, and New Yorkers had to wonder where their next Subway Series was coming from. (As an obviously minor historical note, there have been three other local or regional World Series outside New York: the Chicago White Sox beating the Cubs in 1906, the St. Louis Cardinals beating the Browns in 1944 and the Oakland A's beating the San Francisco Giants in 1989. However, the general consensus of New Yorkers to this trivial hinterlands detail is: "Echhh?" Which means exactly what it sounds like.)

For four years, there was no National League baseball in New York at all, but in 1962 the New York Mets were formed in a cruelly meager expansion draft. Their new manager was the aforementioned Casey Stengel, still mugging for the camera and tossing off bon mots, creating an instant cadre of hip fans, driven by ingrained loyalty to the old Dodgers and Giants. The Mets played their first two seasons in the rusting old Polo Grounds, but in 1964 they relocated to a new stadium in Queens, on the site of a former garbage dump that F. Scott Fitzgerald had called the Valley of the Ashes in his novel "The Great Gatsby."

The Mets lived up to their new home, giving no early hope of ever being respectable enough to reach mediocrity, much less a Subway Series.

That's the thing about New York. Its pizza and its bagels and its good teams are unassailably the best on the face of the earth whereas its civil servants, its potholes and its bad teams are unquestionably the worst.

The Mets generally fell into that latter category, although they somehow managed to win

**Al Gionfriddo's legendary catch to rob Joe DiMaggio of a home run in the sixth game of the 1947 World Series raised the hopes of desperate Brooklyn fans, who sadly had to accept defeat yet again to the hated Yankees in the seventh game.**

Yogi Berra is ubiquitous in World Series history, jumping into Don Larsen's arms after Larsen's perfect game in the 1956 Series (right), and vainly trying to prevent Jackie Robinson from stealing home (opposite) in the 1955 Subway Series that produced Brooklyn's one and only world championship.

pennants in 1969—with the retired Stengel in jubilant attendance—and 1973 and 1986 in years when the Yankees were taking a breather from all that Champagne-spraying.

Meanwhile, the legend of the Subway Series grew and grew. Yuppies were transported in from yuppie breeding grounds and became instant New Yorkers, immediately trying to order a Subway Series on the Web. Men arrived from Malawi to sell wristwatches on street corners, but stocked up on Mets-Yankees paraphernalia for that great day a-coming.

In 1999, the Mets came close, frightening Atlanta in the National League championships, while the Yankees went on to win yet another World Series, in four straight games over the Braves.

Everybody in New York, even Yankee fans, solemnly agreed that the Mets would surely have shown more gumption than the Braves did. The sheer noive of New Yorkers would have been worth a game or two to the Mets.

The Subway Series was finally resurrected in 2000, with both teams not beneficiaries of divine providence but rather enriched by local cable-television income. Most of the old hatreds had dissipated decades earlier. Giant fans and Dodger fans had truly hated each other, and united only in their contempt of the Yankees. It was different now.

By 2000, television exposure and television money had turned the players into performers, corporate entities with personal Web sites, freelancers, millionaires, lodge brothers, celebrities.

Also, the rivalry between the Mets and Yankees had been tempered by regular mid-summer games due to the modern gimmick of interleague play. Back in the old days of the Subway Series, the Dodgers or Giants might play the odd exhibition against the Yankees but would never meet them officially until the World Series. Contact during the regular season between the Yanks and Mets tended to raise the respect for the other side.

It was hard for a Met fan to hate a Yankee team with the charismatic Derek Jeter, the serene Bernie Williams, the mysterious Cuban refugee Orlando (El Duque) Hernandez. It was hard for a Yankee fan to hate a Met team with the exuberant Al Leiter, the quiet Edgardo Alfonzo, the home-boy reliever John Franco, son of a Brooklyn sanitation worker.

Anticipating the Subway Series, there was the normal high quotient of New York extravagance—tabloid fever, special subway trains, T-shirt capitalism, talk-radio babble, even Mayor Rudolph W. Giuliani lurking at far too many Yankee functions in his ubiquitous Yankee jacket. (Who was watching the store?)

New Yorkers were not to be disappointed, as the two teams came up with long games, taut games and heavy doses of anger, danger, name-calling, resentments and all the other good things that enrich life in Gotham. New Yorkers were convinced they deserved the Subway Series—as long as there were no more of these humiliating 44-year intervals. The noive.

# The Regular Season

# Kings in Queens

By **TYLER KEPNER**

The Mets were greatly aided by offseason acquisitions like Mike Hampton (right), who won 15 games and was particularly effective in the late season, and by the emergence of new young stars like Benny Agbayani (left), who batted .289 and drove in 60 runs in 119 games.

### STANDINGS
### ALL-STAR BREAK

#### EASTERN DIVISION

| Team | Won | Lost | Pct. | GB |
|---|---|---|---|---|
| Atlanta | 52 | 36 | .591 | – |
| New York | 48 | 38 | .558 | 3 |
| Florida | 45 | 43 | .511 | 7 |
| Montreal | 42 | 42 | .500 | 8 |
| Philadelphia | 39 | 47 | .453 | 12 |

#### CENTRAL DIVISION

| Team | Won | Lost | Pct. | GB |
|---|---|---|---|---|
| St. Louis | 51 | 36 | .586 | – |
| Cincinnati | 43 | 44 | .494 | 8 |
| Pittsburgh | 38 | 48 | .442 | 12½ |
| Milwaukee | 37 | 51 | .420 | 14½ |
| Chicago | 35 | 52 | .407 | 15½ |
| Houston | 30 | 57 | .345 | 21 |

#### WESTERN DIVISION

| Team | Won | Lost | Pct. | GB |
|---|---|---|---|---|
| Arizona | 51 | 37 | .580 | – |
| San Francisco | 46 | 39 | .541 | 3½ |
| Colorado | 45 | 40 | .529 | 4½ |
| Los Angeles | 44 | 42 | .512 | 6 |
| San Diego | 38 | 49 | .437 | 12½ |

Before his 13th year as a major league manager, Bobby Valentine did something he'd never done before. He decided to save every lineup card of the season.

"I think we're going to have a special year," Valentine told his bench coach, John Stearns.

It was a special time for the Mets, and the first two games foretold the season to come: high drama, delicious controversy and mixed results.

The Mets and Cubs met in Tokyo and split a two-game series that featured nine walks by Mike Hampton, a game-winning grand slam in the 11th inning by Benny Agbayani and an implied threat to fight Valentine by the Cubs manager, Don Baylor.

That fight never happened, but by mid-April, Valentine was in a fight for his job after a controversial speech to graduate students in Philadelphia. Mets General Manager Steve Phillips confronted Valentine, who survived to complete the final year on his contract. But Valentine's unresolved contract status was a constant distraction.

The Mets eliminated another side issue when they released the unhappy and unproductive outfielder Rickey Henderson in mid-May. With Henderson gone and Darryl Hamil-

ton injured, the Mets gave the young players Agbayani and Jay Payton regular playing time and watched both enjoy strong seasons.

Hampton, the Mets' major off-season acquisition, and closer Armando Benitez struggled through early May but dominated thereafter, Benitez setting a club record with 41 saves. The veteran pitchers Al Leiter (16-8) and John Franco provided consistency.

Mike Piazza and Edgardo Alfonzo paced the offense. Both batted .324, with Piazza the team leader in homers (38) and runs batted in (113), Alfonzo first in runs scored (109). Alfonzo committed only 10 errors, bringing stability to an infield that lost the Gold Glove shortstop Rey Ordonez to a broken left forearm in May.

After a distressing weekend in Atlanta in late July, in which the Mets lost two of three to their National League East nemesis, the Mets surged. They won 26 of 36 games starting July 25, prevailing over and over in close, low-scoring games. They entered September alone in first place for the first time since 1990.

Then they stumbled. Swept in St. Louis at the start of the month, the Mets dropped 12 of their first 18 games in September. Their offense disappeared, and so did their magic—the Mets had scored 10 runs in the eighth inning of a comeback victory over Atlanta in June, but by September the Braves looked dominant.

On Sept. 26, the Braves clinched the division at Shea Stadium. It was the Braves' seventh victory in 11 games with the Mets. The next night, Rick Reed pitched the Mets to a victory that clinched the wild card. The Mets won their next four games, and entered the playoffs to meet the N.L. West champ for the second year in a row.

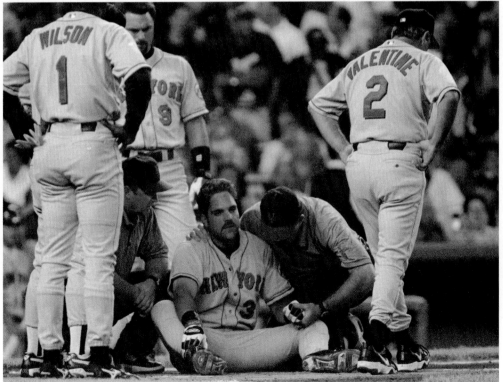

# A Season of Change

By **BUSTER OLNEY**

The Yankees' manager, Joe Torre, has always admired the way his team has rammed its way through the regular season, in spite of family illnesses or illnesses within the team. But in mid-June, his players seemed entirely distracted, Torre thought; the team was not playing well and there were on-going trade talks, the likable and sensitive Ricky Ledee in the middle of all of them. Ledee would go online at night and read the latest rumors, and then monitor a chat room on the Yankees' Web site to see what nasty things were being said about him, words that saddened him. The Yankees were 38–35 when they finally traded Ledee and a couple of minor leaguers to Cleveland for David Justice, and with the help of Justice and seven other significant additions, the Yankees finally seized control of the American League East, winning 44 of their next 67 games. Justice slugged 41 homers, 20 of them for the Yankees. The left-hander Denny Neagle was acquired from Cincinnati and stabi-

Derek Jeter (opposite) turned in his third consecutive season with 200 hits or more; Andy Pettitte (left) survived early-season shakiness to become perhaps the Yankees' most reliable starter.

| STANDINGS | | | |
|---|---|---|---|
| ALL-STAR BREAK | | | |
| **EASTERN DIVISION** | | | |
| Team | Won | Lost | Pct. | GB |
| New York . . . . . . .45 | 38 | .542 | – |
| Toronto . . . . . . . .48 | 41 | .539 | – |
| Boston . . . . . . . .43 | 41 | .512 | 2½ |
| Baltimore . . . . . .38 | 48 | .442 | 8½ |
| Tampa Bay . . . . .34 | 51 | .400 | 12 |
| **CENTRAL DIVISION** | | | |
| Team | Won | Lost | Pct. | GB |
| Chicago . . . . . . .55 | 32 | .632 | – |
| Cleveland . . . . . .44 | 42 | .512 | 10½ |
| Kansas City . . . .39 | 46 | .459 | 15 |
| Detroit . . . . . . . .38 | 46 | .452 | 15½ |
| Minnesota . . . . .38 | 52 | .422 | 18½ |
| **WESTERN DIVISION** | | | |
| Team | Won | Lost | Pct. | GB |
| Seattle . . . . . . . .51 | 35 | .593 | – |
| Oakland . . . . . . .48 | 38 | .558 | 3 |
| Anaheim . . . . . . .47 | 41 | .534 | 5 |
| Texas . . . . . . . . .42 | 43 | .494 | 8½ |

Midsummer's dream: David Justice (opposite) came from Cleveland and provided instant offense; as the season wore on Roger Clemens (left) began pitching with his old fire.

lized the rotation for two months, and Glenallen Hill, a reserve outfielder with the Cubs, was added and hammered 10 homers in his first 51 at-bats. The Yankees had gambled that Jorge Posada would be ready to take over as the full-time catcher, and Posada rewarded them with 28 homers, 107 walks and 86 runs batted in. Bernie Williams was an m.v.p. candidate until he was injured in August. The shortstop Derek Jeter finished the year with 201 hits. Roger Clemens and Andy Pettitte pitched exceptionally in the second half of the season. The Yankees went into Boston with a six-game lead on Sept. 8, a make-or-break series for the Red Sox. Clemens shut out the Red Sox for eight innings on Friday night, in a 4–0 victory, and on Saturday, Scott Brosius

clubbed a three-run homer in the seventh inning off the Cy Young Award–winner Pedro Martinez, ensuring Boston would not gain ground over the weekend. With David Cone nursing a dislocated shoulder at the end of his miserable 4–14 season, Torre tabbed the rookie left-hander Randy Keisler to pitch the final game of the series, and Keisler—making his major-league debut—held Boston to one run over five innings and was the winning pitcher as the Yankees all but buried the Red Sox, increasing their lead to nine games. Those moments in Boston, they all agreed later, were when the Yankees knew for sure, in spite of all those mid-season distractions, that they were headed to the playoffs for the sixth straight year.

| STANDINGS | | | | |
|---|---|---|---|---|
| END OF SEASON | | | | |
| EASTERN DIVISION | | | | |
| Team | Won | Lost | Pct. | GB |
| New York ...... | 87 | 74 | .540 | – |
| Boston ........ | 85 | 77 | .525 | 2½ |
| Toronto ........ | 83 | 79 | .512 | 4½ |
| Baltimore ...... | 74 | 88 | .457 | 13½ |
| Tampa Bay ..... | 69 | 92 | .429 | 18 |
| CENTRAL DIVISION | | | | |
| Team | Won | Lost | Pct. | GB |
| Chicago ....... | 95 | 67 | .586 | – |
| Cleveland ..... | 90 | 72 | .556 | 5 |
| Detroit ........ | 79 | 83 | .488 | 16 |
| Kansas City .... | 77 | 85 | .475 | 18 |
| Minnesota ..... | 69 | 93 | .426 | 26 |
| WESTERN DIVISION | | | | |
| Team | Won | Lost | Pct. | GB |
| Oakland ........ | 91 | 70 | .565 | – |
| Seattle ........ | 91 | 71 | .562 | ½ |
| Anaheim ...... | 82 | 80 | .506 | 9½ |
| Texas ......... | 71 | 91 | .438 | 20½ |

# The Playoffs

# A Pennant in Shea

By **TYLER KEPNER**

**Something old, something new: In their run through the playoffs, the Mets got clutch performances from Edgardo Alfonzo (right) and unanticipated brilliance from the rookie Timo Perez (left), who entered the playoffs with a total of just 49 major-league at-bats.**

The Mets were not sure they would even celebrate their entry into the playoffs. They were far behind the Braves in the National League East standing, but a victory over Atlanta on Sept. 26 would clinch at least a wild-card berth. General Manager Steve Phillips made it clear: there would be no post-game party if the division title was still at stake.

The Braves took care of that by beating the Mets at Shea Stadium that night to clinch the division. When the Mets won the next night, they ensured themselves of consecutive playoff appearances for the first time in their 39-year history. The Champagne flowed.

A drenched Mike Piazza stood in the middle of it all and offered a telling insight for October: "I think every team in the playoffs in this league has, at one time, been the best team in the league. The team that's able to recapture that form is the one that's going to win."

The Mets would become that team, winning seven of nine games in the playoffs to capture their first N.L. pennant since 1986.

Before the first pitch of their first-round series, the Mets were energized by the shock-

**Mike Piazza, always a vital cog in the Mets offense, hit a sizzling .412 against the Cardinals in the N.L.C.S.**

the kind of spirit and abandon that marks them in their best times.

The players believed that their Game 2 victory in San Francisco was the pivotal moment of the playoffs. It gave them a split of the first two games in a park where they had never won, and they were inspired by their perseverance in coming back after blowing a three-run lead in the ninth inning.

Game 2 also featured the introduction of Timo Perez to the Mets' starting lineup. Right fielder Derek Bell, who led the team in at-bats during the regular season, suffered a serious ankle injury in Game 1. Perez, who had the fewest at-bats of any position player on the postseason roster, replaced Bell the next day, batting leadoff.

He was a revelation. Signed for less than $100,000 out of the Japanese minor leagues, the 23-year-old native of the Dominican Republic sparked the Mets over and over. Perez was daring, bunting for a single with two strikes in Game 2 at San Francisco, and clutch: nine times in the eight games he started over two National League playoff rounds, Perez had the first hit of a run-scoring rally.

"I'm going to give him a big kiss when I see him," said Bell, who watched most of the playoffs from his home in Tampa. "I knew he could play."

The Mets always knew Edgardo Alfonzo could play, but in his second appearance on the playoff stage, he may have finally convinced the nation that he is a superstar. Batting second in Bell's absence, Alfonzo thrived in tandem with Perez, and he knocked in five runs to lead the Mets to a four-game series victory over the Giants.

Alfonzo was even better in the N.L.C.S. against the Cardinals, batting .444 and solidifying his status as a team leader. "When we get in a situation where we need a hit, where we need a guy to come through, everybody on this team wants Fonzie at the plate," said outfielder Darryl Hamilton.

Alfonzo was one of several home-grown Mets who produced. Jay Payton had game-winning singles in Game 2 of the division series and the N.L.C.S., Benny Agbayani hit safely in every game of the first two rounds and starter Bobby J. Jones threw a one-hitter against the Giants.

ing developments in the other N.L. Division Series. The Braves, who had played in every N.L.C.S. since 1991, were losing their second game to the St. Louis Cardinals. The N.L. Central champions went on to sweep the Braves, eliminating a foe that had a stranglehold on the Mets for years.

"It was really refreshing that we didn't have to play the Braves," reliever Turk Wendell said. "That's something that really uplifted the team."

After losing the opening game of the playoffs to the National League West-champion San Francisco Giants, the Mets played with

ing himself under a fly ball by Rick Wilkins. The Mets would be bound for the World Series in a moment, but Perez could not wait to start celebrating, waving his arms and jumping for joy as the ball tumbled toward him. Finally, it landed in his glove, and the new National League champions swarmed Hampton behind the mound. As he walked through a stadium tunnel minutes later, the team's co-owner, Fred Wilpon, spotted some reporters and tapped one on the shoulder.

Wilpon had said in spring training that he expected the Mets to do better than they had in 1999, when the Braves beat them in the N.L.C.S. Now, the team had fulfilled his mission. "We went one further," Wilpon said, smiling. Then he entered a clubhouse that had not seen such joy in 14 years.

**With Mike Hampton (left) in complete command in a pair of victories over the Cardinals, Bobby Valentine (above) had good reason to smile.**

The Mets' expensive imports paid off mostly in the Cardinals series. Piazza hit .412, with two homers. Todd Zeile had eight runs batted in. Robin Ventura had big hits in the final two games, and Mike Hampton earned the m.v.p. award with two dominating performances.

Hampton, acquired to be the Mets' ace in an off-season trade with Houston, tossed seven shutout innings in Game 1, then blanked the Cardinals, 7-0, in the Game 5 finale.

Fittingly, Perez caught the last out, camp-

# Giant Slayers

By **TYLER KEPNER**

**Molto Benny: An epic Game 3 ended in the 13th inning, when Benny Agbayani (right) blasted a game-winning home run over the left-field fence, to the delight of the Shea faithful and his welcoming teammates (opposite).**

The last time the Mets had visited Pacific Bell Park, the sparkling new field bordering San Francisco Bay, their failures had propelled the Giants to a dream season. Starting with a four-game sweep of the Mets in May, the Giants won 54 of their last 73 home games. Over all, the Giants won 97 games, the most in the majors.

In October, the Mets' sluggish start to the Division Series nearly lifted the Giants again. In Game 1, Mike Hampton gave up four runs in the third inning, one on a Barry Bonds triple and three on a homer by Ellis Burks that struck the left-field foul pole.

The Giants led by 5–1, and the score did not change as Livan Hernandez and two relievers mastered the Mets.

Game 2 could have been a disaster for the Mets. Trying to protect a 4–1 lead, closer Armando Benitez gave up a three-run homer to the Giants pinch-hitter J.T. Snow with one out in the ninth. The score was tied, the crowd was ecstatic and the momentum belonged to the Giants.

But with two outs in the top of the 10th, Darryl Hamilton pinch hit against Giants reliever Felix Rodriguez. Hamilton had been

offended in Game 1 when Rodriguez danced off the mound after fanning him with the bases loaded. With what he said was the greatest focus of his 12-year career, Hamilton doubled and scored the go-ahead run when Jay Payton singled him home.

John Franco relieved Benitez in the 10th, and with two outs and two strikes on Bonds, he shook off catcher Mike Piazza's call for a fastball. Choosing his signature pitch, the change-up, Franco struck out Bonds looking and the Mets headed home with a 5–4 victory and a 1–1 tie in the series.

The game had become a battle of bullpens, and the Mets outlasted the Giants with five relievers combining for seven shutout innings. Benny Agbayani pounded an Aaron Fultz fastball into the left-field bleachers with one out in the 13th, giving the Mets a 3–2 victory and a 2–1 lead in the series.

For Game 4, the Mets turned to Bobby J. Jones, knowing that a loss would send them on an overnight flight to San Francisco for a decisive fifth game. Instead, Jones responded with the performance of his career.

He got an early lead on a two-run homer

**Bobby J. Jones (above) was brilliant in Game 4, allowing only one hit and three baserunners overall; a first-inning two-run home run from Robin Ventura (above, right) was all he needed in the 4–0 series-clinching victory.**

The third game was a 5-hour-23-minute, 13-inning thrill ride that started dismally for the Mets but ended in euphoria.

They had no hits until the sixth, when Hamilton singled. Timo Perez—playing for Derek Bell, who sprained his ankle severely in Game 1—drove Hamilton in with a single, but the Mets trailed by 2–1 when Giants closer Robb Nen came in with two outs in the eighth.

On Nen's first pitch, Lenny Harris—who had reached on a close call at first base—stole second. Harris scored on a double by Edgardo Alfonzo, tying the game, 2–2, and giving Nen his first blown save in more than four months.

by Robin Ventura in the first inning. Jones retired the first 12 Giants he faced, but Jeff Kent led off the fifth with a double and two walks loaded the bases with two outs. With his bullpen depleted from the night before, Manager Dusty Baker allowed pitcher Mark Gardner to bat.

Gardner popped out, ending the inning, and the Mets knocked him out in the bottom of the fifth when doubles by Perez and Alfonzo brought in two runs.

Spotting his fastball with precision and using a biting curve—"textbook pitching," Piazza said—Jones retired the side in order in eight of nine innings in a 4–0, series-

clinching victory. It was the first complete-game, one-hit shutout in the postseason since Jim Lonborg did it for Boston in the 1967 World Series.

Bonds, who hit .176 in the series, flied to Payton in center for the final out. Jones, usually the most reserved Met, let himself enjoy the moment, as Piazza lifted him up and Ventura leaped excitedly onto his back. When Jones returned to the clubhouse after several rounds of interviews, his teammates greeted him by chanting his name and dousing him in Champagne.

Moments later, Ventura sneaked up behind the pitcher, carrying Jones's 4-year-old son,

Breyton, on his shoulders. The boy poured bubbly all over his father's head, and Jones smiled broadly, kissing his son. It was a satisfying moment for an eight-year Met who was left off the postseason roster in '99 and was sent to Class AAA Norfolk after struggling early in 2000.

"After what I went through in the beginning of the season," Jones said, "to battle back and have a chance to do something in the postseason—it meant a lot."

For the second year in a row, the Mets would play for the National League pennant, with a new opponent—the St. Louis Cardinals—on deck.

**The Agony and the Ecstasy: With the Mets celebration already underway, a disappointed Barry Bonds, who hit a meager .176 in the series, jogged off the field after flying out to end Game 4.**

# Hampton's Escape Act

Starting strong: Mike Piazza (opposite) drove in the first Mets run with a first-inning double; Robin Ventura followed with a sacrifice fly that scored Edgardo Alfonzo (right) with the second.

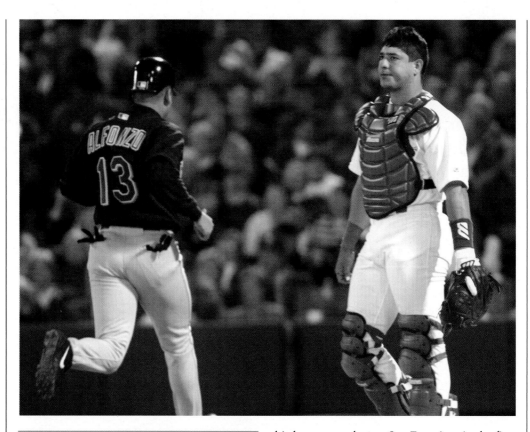

| LINE SCORE | | | |
|---|---|---|---|
| New York | 2 0 0 | 0 1 0 | 0 0 3 | –6 |
| St. Louis | 0 0 0 | 0 0 0 | 0 0 2 | –2 |

ST. LOUIS—Mike Hampton made these the first words of his postgame news conference tonight: "It wasn't pretty." His manager, Bobby Valentine, opened with these: "His performance was fabulous."

Hampton is a perfectionist, and his seven shutout innings looked fine to the Mets, who rode them to a 6–2 victory over the St. Louis Cardinals in the first game of the National League Championship Series.

But Hampton knew he had better stuff in his last start, a loss at San Francisco in the first game of the last playoff round. One bad pitch cost him the game that day, but overall, he felt his command was better, his pitches sharper. He encountered plenty of trouble tonight, but escaped every time. It was a maximum-effort performance, he said, and it was draining.

"There was only one inning when I retired the side in order," Hampton said, "so there were always people on base, and every pitch had some meaning behind it."

Hampton, who lost in the division series and did not have a victory in three postseason starts for Houston, allowed six hits and walked four. John Franco followed with a scoreless

ber, Leiter said, is whether the pitcher works out of it. "Certainly Mike had his moments," Leiter said, "but really what it is is mental toughness and making quality pitches when he had to, and he did that."

The most crucial pitch for Hampton was his last one, to Jim Edmonds with two out and two runners on in the seventh. Hampton threw a cutter away, and Edmonds bashed it to left, trotting to first and tracking the flight of the ball and Benny Agbayani's uncertain pursuit of it.

The wind blowing his way, Agbayani retreated tentatively to the warning track. With his glove about shoulder-high, Agbayani cradled the ball. The Mets' 3–0 lead was preserved.

"I think everybody took a deep breath after that catch," Agbayani said. "Some of the guys in the dugout said, 'You made us nervous there.'"

That was the Cardinals' last, best chance against Hampton. If Shawon Dunston had reached base against Franco with a runner on and two out in the eighth, Mark McGwire would have come to bat as the potential tying run. But Franco retired Dunston on a fly ball, and the Mets scored three runs in the ninth off reliever Mike James, who allowed a homer to Todd Zeile, a single to Agbayani and a two-run homer to Jay Payton. Many of the 52,255 fans left Busch Stadium then.

In their three division series victories, the Mets scored in seven innings. Perez had a hit in four of those rallies, and he was involved in the first two tonight. The rookie leadoff hitter is a force, and the Mets readily acknowledge the difference he makes.

"We didn't have a prototypical leadoff hitter, and we do in Timo," said Agbayani, who was displaced at the top of the order by Perez. "He gets on base, has some power, and you've

**John Franco twirled a scoreless eighth inning, retiring Shawon Dunston to avoid a possible confrontation with Mark McGwire; Todd Zeile (opposite) gave the Mets a little more breathing room with a solo home run off Mike James in the ninth.**

inning. Before the Cardinals scored a pair of unearned runs in the ninth, the Mets' pitchers had tossed 26 consecutive scoreless innings.

Hampton held the Cardinals hitless in seven at-bats with runners in scoring position. His counterpart, the 20-game winner Darryl Kile, pitched well over seven innings, but was burned by the top of the Mets' batting order. Mike Piazza drove in the first run with a double, Edgardo Alfonzo scored a run and drove in another, and Timo Perez figured in both of the first two rallies.

Even in the best-pitched games, said Al Leiter, who starts Game 2 for the Mets on Thursday, there are one or two moments when a pitcher gets in trouble. The difference in Octo-

got one of the best clutch hitters in baseball hitting second. If Timo gets on, you know Fonzie's going to make something happen."

That was the pattern against the Giants, and it continued tonight. Perez led off the game with a double to the right-field corner, and with Alfonzo batting, Kile's fastball skipped away from the catcher, allowing Perez to go to third. Then Alfonzo walked, and Piazza came to bat.

Piazza has made a habit of hitting well against the best pitchers, and he came in with a .344 career average against Kile. On the first pitch, Piazza pulled a curveball inside the third-base line for a double, bringing in Perez with the game's first run. Robin Ventura then lined out to left field, deep enough to score Alfonzo to put the Mets ahead by 2–0. Piazza was still on second as Zeile, who also hits Kile well, came to bat. But Zeile struck out looking on a pitch he thought was inside, and Agbayani grounded out, ending the inning.

Hampton nearly surrendered the lead in the bottom of the inning, and he said he was conscious of the Cardinals' big first inning in Game 1 of their division series, when they battered Atlanta's Greg Maddux for six runs, propelling them to a sweep.

With two outs, Eric Davis, a nemesis of Hampton who was batting cleanup to take advantage of the matchup, singled, then Will Clark walked. The bases were loaded for Carlos Hernandez, and Hampton went with his best pitch, a sinker.

"I didn't want to leave a ball over the plate; I didn't want to give in," Hampton said. "I wanted to stay aggressive."

It worked, as Hernandez grounded into a fielder's choice, ending the inning and sending Hampton on his way to that elusive first postseason victory.

"It's good to finally win a game," Hampton said. "I'm not going to downplay that. But it's really about having a quality start, giving the team a chance to win."

Ugly or fabulous, great stuff or not, Hampton did that tonight, and the Mets are three victories from the World Series.

# Youth Movement

Though the veteran Mike Piazza (right) contributed a solo home run in the third inning, the Mets victory was largely generated by the team's younger players, including rookie Timo Perez, who scored a run and made several sterling plays in the outfield, including a sliding catch in the third inning (opposite).

| LINE SCORE | | | | | | | | | |
|---|---|---|---|---|---|---|---|---|---|
| **New York** | 2 0 1 | 0 0 0 | 0 2 1 | –6 |
| **St. Louis** | 0 1 0 | 0 2 0 | 0 2 0 | –5 |

ST. LOUIS—The Mets were built to win this season. That was the mandate from ownership, and that is why the roster is loaded with veterans. In the grand plan, no rookies figured to play any significant roles.

But sometimes a veteran starter cannot hold an early lead. Sometimes, veteran relievers crumble in the late innings. The Mets' youth delivered tonight, when two rookies, Jay Payton and Timo Perez, sparked them to a 6–5 victory over the St. Louis Cardinals and a commanding 2–0 lead in the National League Championship Series.

Payton singled in the pinch-runner Joe McEwing in the top of the ninth inning, breaking a 5–5 tie and becoming the hero after going hitless in his first three at-bats, stranding three runners.

"There's no one on the team, maybe no one in the league, who has as much confidence in himself as Jay Payton," Mets Manager Bobby Valentine said. "He didn't have any hits going into that at-bat, but I know he believed deep down in his heart, right down to his toes, that he was the best man in that situation."

Payton gave credit to the veterans who surrounded him, notably Edgardo Alfonzo, whose eighth-inning single scored the rookie Timo Perez from first and gave the Mets a lead they later gave up.

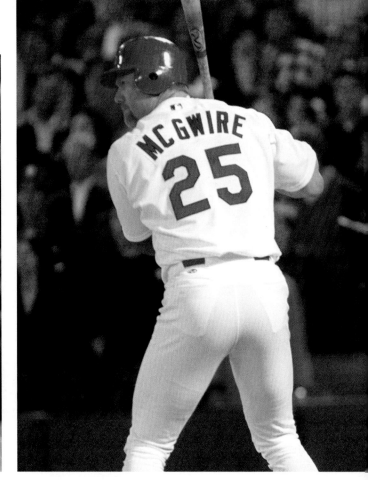

**Al Leiter (above) pitched well but left the game after the seventh inning with the score tied at 3; fortunately for the Mets, Mark McGwire's only appearance (above, middle) came in an obvious intentional-walk situation.**

"I watch Fonzie, and to me, he's my m.v.p.," Payton said. "He comes up with big hits. I want to go out there and try to help my team and do the same thing."

The game finished one minute short of four hours, making it the longest nine-inning game in N.L.C.S. history. The Mets fought for every minute of it, which every team tries to do but which the Mets always seem to pull off.

"That has something to do with the unity of this team," said first baseman Todd Zeile, who was 2 for 3 with two runs batted in. "We're not relying on one particular guy, so you've got everyone pulling for everyone else.

"But there's got to be more than that. A lot of guys in this room have great spirit and a lot of fight to them. We've played games like this so many times and had so much success, it gives us confidence that when our backs are against the wall, we're going to respond."

The Mets got a 2–0 lead in the first inning, but the Cardinals fought back against Al Leiter to tie the score at 3-3 through seven. In the eighth, Perez slapped a single with two outs and scored from first on another single, by Alfonzo, putting the Mets ahead, 4–3.

They scored another run, but the Cardinals

pulled even with a pair of runs off John Franco in the bottom of the eighth. Mike Timlin, the Cardinals' fifth reliever, came on in the ninth, and Robin Ventura reached base when first baseman Will Clark could not handle his bouncer. It went for an error, and Ventura advanced to second when Benny Agbayani put down a sacrifice bunt—something he did not do once in the regular season.

McEwing ran for Ventura, and Payton smashed a single to center, the ball eluding the Gold Glover Jim Edmonds and bouncing over his head as McEwing dashed in for the winning run. Turk Wendell earned the victory.

Mets relievers had allowed only two earned runs in 13⅔ innings this postseason. They equaled that in the bottom of the eighth, when Franco and Wendell gave up the lead. Carlos Hernandez walked with one out, and Clark singled. A wild pitch from Franco brought in one run, and Wendell relieved Franco with two out.

When the announced pinch-hitter, Placido Polanco, sat down, a buzz rippled through the 52,250 fans. The injured slugger Mark McGwire, they sensed, would come up.

Instead, J. D. Drew came to bat, and he

Jay Payton (left),
0 for 3 entering the ninth
inning, came through
in the clutch, driving
home Joe McEwing with
the winning run.

made the fans cheer, anyway. Drew drove a double to right center, bringing in Clark with the tying run. Now it was time for McGwire, who is hitless in eight career at-bats off Wendell.

The crowd roared and the flashbulbs popped. Then, Valentine ordered an intentional walk.

It was the right move: Wendell fanned the next hitter, Craig Paquette, sending the game to the ninth inning tied, 5-5.

Wendell said he was shocked McGwire would bat in an obvious situation for an intentional walk.

"I was totally surprised," Wendell said. "Obviously, you just throw four pitches to him, walk him and go after the next guy. I give Tony La Russa a lot more credit than that. Obviously we were going to walk him. Why not pull him back and send somebody else up there?"

La Russa, the Cardinals' manager, said he was down to only one other bench player, the little-used catcher Rick Wilkins.

The only move La Russa said he may regret was starting the 21-year-old rookie Rick Ankiel, who was dreadful and left in the first inning.

"He said something about how he didn't feel the baseball, but it's the manager's respon-

sibility to put guys in the right position," La Russa said. "I blame myself. I don't blame Rick Ankiel—he's too special."

There were no indications early that the game would become so close. The Mets pushed across two runs in the first off Ankiel, who suffered another postseason implosion.

Ankiel, who threw five wild pitches in his division series start against the Atlanta Braves, fired his first pitch to the backstop, over Perez's head, and the crowd stirred.

Was Ankiel trying to incite the Mets, whose general manager, Steve Phillips, said the Cardinals' Mike James had thrown at Mike Bordick in Game 1?

It quickly became obvious Ankiel could not put a pitch where he wanted it. Of his first 20 pitches, five went to the backstop and two were wild pitches. He allowed two runs before Britt Reames came in with four and a third innings of solid relief.

Reames allowed only one run, an opposite-field leadoff homer in the third to Piazza, who was happier spreading credit to the rookies.

"It's great to see Jay and Timo and the guys come through for us and execute," Piazza said. "They want to be up there in those situations."

# Knocked Down

Edgar Renteria (opposite) received first-inning congratulations from Fernando Vina (4) after scoring the second of five runs the Cardinals manufactured off Mets starter Rick Reed; three innings later Reed was in the dugout (right) taking his frustration out on the Gatorade bucket.

| LINE SCORE | | | | | | | | | | |
|---|---|---|---|---|---|---|---|---|---|---|
| **St. Louis** | 2 | 0 | 2 | 1 | 3 | 0 | 0 | 0 | 0 | –8 |
| **New York** | 1 | 0 | 0 | 1 | 0 | 0 | 0 | 0 | 0 | –2 |

NEW YORK—The St. Louis Cardinals came out swinging, the Mets went down looking, and the National League Championship Series suddenly has a very different feel to it.

The Mets mounted a desperate rally in the ninth inning of Game 3 today, putting two runners on and forcing Cardinals Manager Tony La Russa to use his closer, Dave Veres, to protect a six-run lead. Veres faced three Mets, and all took called third strikes.

It was an apt conclusion to an 8–2 Cardinals victory in which the Mets absorbed all the body blows and never got up off the mat. They scored both of their runs on double plays.

"Every time we punched back," first baseman Todd Zeile said, "they punched back twice."

After losing the first two games of the series at home, the Cardinals littered Shea Stadium with 14 hits. Mets outfielder Darryl Hamilton, who flied out to stifle a potential rally in the fourth inning, said: "We never thought this series was going to be easy, and it's not. There's a long way to go. It'd be great to go and win four in a row, but that doesn't happen very often."

Rick Reed sustained most of the pounding, allowing eight hits and five runs over three and

a third innings. When he left the game trailing by 5–1, he fired his glove against the dugout wall, slapped a paper cup off the Gatorade bucket and retreated to the clubhouse.

There was not much left to see besides the dominance of Cardinals starter Andy Benes, who held the Mets to six hits and two runs over eight innings. The only Met with two hits off Benes was Edgardo Alfonzo, who extended his postseason hitting streak to nine games, a club record.

Benes was throwing to Carlos Hernandez, who came to St. Louis in a midseason trade. Because he was not familiar with him, Hernandez got Benes out of his pattern of mainly throwing fastballs. The Mets were flummoxed.

"Some pitchers, you can see they change their style and get a little bit more aggressive in the zone when they get a lead," Zeile said. "He didn't. He still picked the corners, used the slider—even 3-2 sliders with an 8–2 lead.

He wasn't going to let himself get out of his game plan, because it had been working."

Reed never got into his. The Cardinals had a .333 average off him in two starts during the regular season, and yesterday even their outs were hard smashes. Reed relies on locating his pitches, and they were up in the strike zone because he was rushing his delivery, something he does perhaps five times a year. "I wish it had waited until spring training," Reed said.

Three batters into the game, the Cardinals had two runs for their first lead of the series. Fernando Vina smacked a leadoff single to left, then Edgar Renteria dropped a bunt in front of Robin Ventura at third. Ventura approached it with his bare hand extended, but reconsidered and tried to glove it. He could not pick up the ball and was charged with an error, and Jim Edmonds followed with a two-run double to the left-field corner.

Will Clark singled on the next pitch, but

Reed recovered, striking out the next three batters. He worked a 1-2-3 second inning, but knew something was wrong.

"My pitches were up," Reed said. "I got away with some pitches that inning, and I just wasn't able to iron it out."

The Cardinals hit Reed hard, scoring twice in the third and once in the fourth before he was pulled with one out and two on. In calling for the left-hander Glendon Rusch, Manager

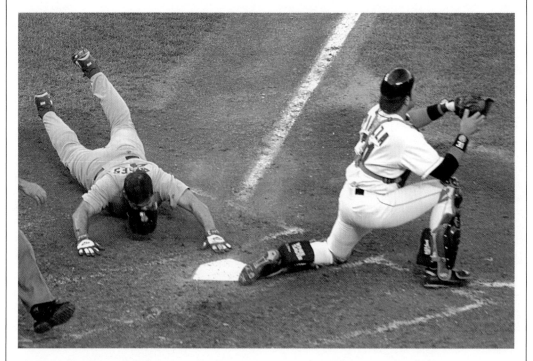

inning where I had bases loaded and I didn't come up with a hit," Payton said. "We got a run and made it 5–2, but we should have come out of that inning with more runs. After that, we didn't really have it, and Benes did a good job."

Rick White came on for the fifth, and Fernando Tatis bashed his first pitch off the plexiglass in front of the left-field bullpen for a double. After that, White tried to establish his breaking pitches because he had seen the Car-

**Both sides now: Mike Piazza (opposite) reached into the stands to grab a foul ball off the bat of J.D. Drew in the third inning, but was unable to prevent a sliding Andy Benes from scoring the Cardinals' fifth run in the fourth (left).**

Bobby Valentine summoned a pitcher who had handled the Cardinals much better than Reed, allowing a .188 average in two starts.

Rusch fanned Edmonds, walked Clark to load the bases, then stared in at Mark McGwire, the sore-kneed slugger limited to pinch-hitting in this series.

Rusch, who has learned to trust his average fastball, buzzed McGwire up and in, then went away. He came inside again and got McGwire to fly out harmlessly to left. "If he hits that up a little more, he probably hits it to the parking lot," Rusch said.

But Rusch had survived, and the only problem was leaving him in. In the bottom of the inning, with a run in on Jay Payton's double-play grounder and runners on first and third, Valentine had to call for Hamilton to pinch-hit for Rusch. When Hamilton flied out, the life went out of the Mets.

"Probably the feeling of going flat was the

dinals pummel Reed's fastballs.

But White was helpless: he had no control of his curveball or slider. Whenever he used them, the pitches drifted over the middle of the plate, and the Cardinals pounded away.

"I'm just glad I didn't give up more than three runs," White said. "Otherwise, everyone would have been sitting there from the fifth inning on, thinking there's no way we can come back."

If the Mets believed they could recover, they did not show it on the field. Benes retired 12 of 13 hitters from the fifth through the eighth, winning for the first time in eight career postseason games.

It was a vital victory for the Cardinals; no team in baseball history has recovered from a 3–0 deficit to win a four-of-seven-game series. The burden of coming back is still on St. Louis, as the Mets reminded themselves.

"We'd rather be us than them at this point," Zeile said.

# Double Vision

The Mets' four-run barrage in the first inning included consecutive doubles from (above, left to right) Timo Perez, Edgardo Alfonzo and Mike Piazza.

**LINE SCORE**

| | | | | | | | | | | | |
|---|---|---|---|---|---|---|---|---|---|---|---|
| St. Louis | 2 | 0 | 0 | 1 | 3 | 0 | 0 | 0 | 0 | –6 |
| New York | 4 | 3 | 0 | 1 | 0 | 2 | 0 | 0 | x | –10 |

NEW YORK—It was his turn in the batting cage, so Edgardo Alfonzo politely removed himself from a conversation with reporters before the fourth game of the National League Championship Series tonight.

"Excuse me," Alfonzo said. "I've got to go kill somebody here."

Alfonzo, the Mets' second baseman, has become more than an on-field warrior. He is a team leader, and he did not like the relaxed atmosphere around the Mets in their blowout loss to the Cardinals in Game 3.

"Our attitude should be more aggressive, from the dugout to the field," he said.

After Game 3, Alfonzo told Todd Pratt, the reserve catcher, that the Mets were playing as if they were down in the series, not up. To Pratt, the message was clear: the Mets' bench players had to show more energy, and they gathered last night and decided to do so.

The Mets got it right this time, playing with passion from the start. They beat the Cardinals, 10–6, at Shea Stadium and now stand one victory from their first National League pennant since 1986.

The Mets were alive on the bench and the diamond. They fell behind, 2–0, in the top of the first inning but stormed back, hammering away at the Cardinals' best pitcher, Darryl Kile, as the players on the bench whooped it up.

"It's a team thing, and they keep things lively," said third baseman Robin Ventura, who hit the fourth of five Met doubles in the first inning. "When stuff starts happening, they react to it. That's how big innings happen."

When Ventura's double drove in Alfonzo and Mike Piazza, 10 Mets burst from the dugout to greet them on the field, embracing the players and the 3–2 lead the Mets had claimed. They would not trail again.

The Cardinals outhit the Mets, 11–9, but the Mets bunched their runs in the early innings to overwhelm St. Louis. The Mets led, 7–2, after two innings, and when starter Bobby J. Jones faltered in the fifth, Glendon

Rusch came on to earn the victory by pitching three scoreless innings.

Piazza had a home run, a double and three runs scored, Ventura knocked in three runs and Timo Perez scored three times. The Mets were unfazed by a situation that had doomed them yesterday.

Three batters into today's game, the Cardinals were ahead by two runs. If there was ever a here-we-go-again moment, it was this, because the Mets had experienced it in their 8–2 loss yesterday. Then, Fernando Vina led off the game with a single, Edgar Renteria reached on a bunt and Jim Edmonds doubled in two runs. Tonight, Vina doubled, Renteria bunted him to second and Edmonds hit a two-run homer.

The Mets' situation could not have been much worse. They were down by two runs and knew they would have to get to Kile early, because he tends to improve as the game goes on.

But Kile was working on three days' rest, a situation in which he has been awful in his career. Mets first baseman Todd Zeile noticed a difference of about four miles an hour off Kile's

fastball, and Kile had to use the pitch, because he was not getting called strikes on his curveball.

The Mets went to work on Kile early in the count. Perez whacked a ground-rule double that bounced over the right-field wall, extending his hitting streak to seven games. Alfonzo ripped the next pitch down the right-field line for another double.

The Mets had closed the gap to 2–1, with Piazza up next. That was especially bad news for Kile, whom Piazza devours. In 35 career at-bats off Kile, Piazza had 13 hits, for a .371 average. He got ahead in the count, 2–0, then extended his arms and did what he does best, stroking a sizzling liner that kept carrying over right fielder J.D Drew's head.

Alfonzo, who thought Drew might make the catch, had to hold up at third. No matter—two pitches later, Ventura doubled both runners in. After Zeile grounded out, Benny Agbayani swung on a 3–0 pitch and blasted a double off the wall in left-center.

The Mets had a 4–2 lead, and their five doubles were the most in one inning in N.L.C.S. history. Zeile, the only Met without a double among the first six hitters, got his in the next inning, when he thumped a hanging curveball into the left-field corner, scoring two runs. Agbayani singled in another run to put the Mets in front by 7–2.

After home runs by Will Clark and Piazza, the Mets had an 8–3 lead when Jones, who

tossed a one-hit shutout in his last start to clinch the division series against the Giants, unraveled in the fifth. He gave up three hits to start the inning, and Manager Bobby Valentine called for Rusch.

"I've said all along that one of the keys to this series was to keep me out of the games," Rusch said. "If I'm coming in, one of our starters is in trouble. Fortunately tonight, I guess, I came in at the right time."

Rusch allowed two of the runners he inherited to score in the fifth, but he worked a scoreless sixth and seventh to turn the game over to the Mets' late-inning tandem of John Franco and Armando Benitez.

The game could have gotten more interest-ing in the sixth. With Ray Lankford on first and two outs, Zeile dived to his right to snare a hard grounder by Carlos Hernandez and then beat the Cardinals' catcher to the bag. With the score 8–6 at the time, the injured slugger Mark McGwire would have pinch hit.

"That was the place to take a shot," Cardi-nals Manager Tony La Russa said. "He was on deck."

Strong defense continued to aid the Mets. In the seventh, Perez ran down a fly ball in the right-field corner and fired in to second to catch Shawon Dunston, who was trying to tag up. Poor defense hampered the Cardinals, who allowed two unearned runs on two errors by Fernando Tatis in the sixth.

The Mets hit well, fielded well and capital-ized on the Cardinals' mistakes. One more game like this, and they can hold up their end of the Subway Series date. They know their attitude will not impede them.

"The key for us is to come in tomorrow and want to put these guys away, and not have that same mentality we had when we were up 2–0," center fielder Jay Payton said. "I don't think that'll be the case. We're up 3–1 now, and none of the guys in here want to go back to St. Louis. I think we'll come in tomor-row with the same mentality we had today, and hopefully that'll carry over."

# Simply Amazin'

Ya gotta believe: With the victory in hand, the Mets, including Mike Piazza and John Franco (middle, left to right respectively) celebrated the franchise's fourth trip to the World Series while the fans at Shea (above) anticipated a matchup with their crosstown rivals.

NEW YORK—All year long, they promised to be Amazin' Again. That was the Mets' vow, and it was everywhere, from the billboards to the pocket schedules. They fell just short of the World Series last year, thrilling and intriguing their fans with comebacks and controversy. This year they fulfilled the pledge.

The Mets are Amazin', and the capital A fits.

The Mets reached the World Series for the fourth time in their 39-year history tonight when Mike Hampton pitched them to a 7–0 victory over the St. Louis Cardinals in the fifth game of the National League Championship Series at Shea Stadium. The Yankees can make the Subway Series a reality for the first time in 44 years with a victory over Seattle tomorrow night at Yankee Stadium.

Fred Wilpon, the Mets' co-owner and a Brooklyn native who pitched batting practice to the Dodgers in the early 1950's, said he would cheer for the Yankees tomorrow night. Wilpon said he was ecstatic for the city, and an admirer of the Yankees, who have 25 World Series titles to the Mets' two.

"All we are," Wilpon said, "is the little guy in Queens trying to emulate the Yankees."

The biggest little guy in Queens last night was Hampton, the 5-foot-10-inch left-hander who won for the second time this series and captured the most valuable player award. He tossed seven shutout innings in Game 1 and went the distance last night, allowing only three hits and striking out eight.

After getting Rick Wilkins to fly to center fielder Timo Perez for the final out, Hampton thrust his arms in the air and was lifted by third baseman Robin Ventura, touching off a long on-field party.

### LINE SCORE

| | | | | | | | | | | | |
|---|---|---|---|---|---|---|---|---|---|---|---|
| St. Louis | 0 | 0 | 0 | 0 | 0 | 0 | 0 | 0 | 0 | – | 0 |
| New York | 3 | 0 | 0 | 3 | 0 | 0 | 1 | 0 | x | – | 7 |

Series m.v.p. Mike Hampton was in command throughout, tossing a dominant three-hit shutout in the most critical game of his career.

Todd Zeile, whose championship series stats included a gaudy .368 batting average and a team-leading eight runs batted in, doubled in the three runs in the fourth inning that put the game out of reach.

The 40-year-old reliever John Franco, who has been with the Mets 11 years and never tasted the World Series, got a ride on his teammates' shoulders, waving a towel and exulting in the moment. Left fielder Benny Agbayani, who has had a season-long love affair with the fans in the left-field seats, ran to them and slapped hands up and down the front row.

Three hours before game time, the veteran reserve Lenny Harris asked Hampton, "Are you ready?"

Hampton, a picture of intensity even in spring training, had a terse reply: "Just give me the ball."

"I knew we weren't going back to St. Louis after that," Harris said. "He wanted the ball at 5:00."

At 11:39, Hampton—who came into this series without a victory in four career postseason starts—had the victory. With 16 shutout innings this series, he also has a permanent place in Mets' lore.

The Amazin' Mets won it all in 1969. The "Ya Gotta Believe" dreamers added a pennant in '73. The 1986 club swaggered its way to a World Series title with the help of a tricky hop. And now come these Mets, Manager Bobby Valentine's collection of expensive veterans and youthful bargains who became just the second wild-card team to reach the World Series since the playoffs expanded in 1995. The other one, the Florida Marlins in 1997, won the Series.

"When you have great players playing great," Valentine said, "it makes my job real easy."

The biggest addition General Manager Steve Phillips gave Valentine this year was Hampton, a 22-game winner for Houston in 1999 who was traded to the Mets last December. Hampton won 15 games in the regular season.

"I really haven't been able to think much about Mets history," Hampton said. "I wanted to come out and pitch a big game. I wanted my team to be right there behind me and I wanted them to have an easy night. I was fortunate—things went my way."

With a runner on first and the Cardinals struggling to get back in the game in the third inning, the slick-fielding Edgardo Alfonzo ranged to his right to snag a ground ball from Fernando Vina before flipping to Mike Bordick at second to quell a potential rally.

The veterans Edgardo Alfonzo, Mike Piazza and Todd Zeile hit safely in every game of the series. So did Perez, the rookie leadoff sensation who had a hit to start a rally every game. But it was the addition of Hampton that probably did the most to elevate the Mets a step further than last year.

"We have some experience; we went through it a year ago," Phillips said. "The other big difference is our pitching is just that tick better than it was a year ago. We're stronger at the front of our rotation, and a little deeper in the bullpen.

"And I know people criticized Bobby down the stretch, and I raised my eyebrow too, about resting guys. But we had fresher legs going into the postseason, and I think it helped."

A tidy game had an ugly confrontation near the end. With Jay Payton batting for the Mets and two outs in the eighth inning, Cardinals right-hander Dave Veres drilled Payton in the head with a 1–2 fastball. Payton, knocked to the ground, bolted up and stalked out to the mound, St. Louis catcher Eli Marrero in front of him all the way.

Both benches and bullpens emptied, and teammates restrained Payton, who had blood trickling down his face and left for a pinch-runner.

The crowd, joyful all night, howled through the fracas, heavily booing Veres, who was allowed to stay in the game and finish the inning. When Veres returned to the dugout, it was as if the party-crasher had been escorted out. The good times resumed as Hampton completed his masterpiece.

Until Payton's beaning, the crowd shook Shea Stadium most in the fourth inning, after a rally sparked, naturally, by Perez, who singled off the foot of the Cardinals' starter, Pat Hentgen. Piazza singled and Ventura walked, bringing up Zeile with the bases loaded.

With a 2–2 count, Zeile crushed a fastball that cut through the chilly air and caught the wind, crashing into the wall in right center and clearing the bases. The Mets led, 6–0, and Zeile punched the air softly with his fist, satisfied with the bedlam he had set off.

Hentgen's night was over, and the pitching change gave the crowd more time to celebrate the championship they sensed. Suddenly, it was Mookie Wilson's dribbler in '86, the Miracle Mets in '69, the Beatles in concert in '65. The old place pulsated, the fans standing and stomping.

It will be alive again next Tuesday, when Shea Stadium plays host to a World Series game for the first time in 14 years.

"It's probably going to be even more incredible than it was in the 1950's," Mayor Rudolph W. Giuliani said. "In the 50's, it happened almost every year; people got blasé. This city is going to be electric."

# Justice Served

By **BUSTER OLNEY**

**Mid-season acquisition David Justice made two huge swings for the Yankees in the A.L.C.S., the first in Game 2 (right), which produced a double to start the Yankees' seven-run rally in the eighth inning, and the second a titanic three-run blast (opposite) against Seattle's Arthur Rhodes in the seventh inning of Game 6.**

The silence in the Yankees' clubhouse after their game in Baltimore Sept. 29 was awkward for everyone. The Orioles had just drubbed them, 13–2—this after four other losses, to Detroit and Tampa Bay—and the Yankees were reeling, and the funny thing was that they had just clinched the division title. They stood there somewhat confused, not sure how they were supposed to react. After all, does a team in the midst of its worst slump in a decade start popping Champagne corks? But Manager Joe Torre said some words, all the right words, assuring his players that they had earned the right to celebrate, that they

had reached the goal—inherent in spring training—of winning the American League East. Derek Jeter grabbed a bottle, and reliever Jeff Nelson followed, and the players began spraying each other and hugging and congratulating each other.

Don Zimmer, the coach who shares whispers with Torre on the Yankees' bench, might be the only person who knows for sure whether Torre said those words for effect, or if he believed them. Zimmer might be the only person who knows whether the September collapse created any doubt in Torre about his team. The Yankees lost 15 of their last 18

**Bernie Williams followed David Justice's double in the eighth inning of A.L.C.S. Game 2 with a solid single to tie the score; after that the floodgates opened and the Yankees put the game out of reach.**

games and their final seven, the worst finishing performance by any playoff-bound team in the history of baseball, and the results of the individual games were harrowing: eight losses of eight or more runs; the Yankees did not even so much as hold a lead at any point in their last nine road games. Paul O'Neill did not hit a home run after Sept. 6, Scott Brosius did not drive in a run after Sept. 10, and the young and old members of the pitching staff floundered: from the 38-year-old Roger Clemens, who allowed six runs in four innings in his last start, to the Class AAA call-ups like Ted Lilly, who was so rattled in one inning that he twice failed to cover bases. On the eve of the playoffs, Torre was asked how the slump might manifest itself, and he did not try to paint a pastoral picture. "We'll find out," he said.

What the Yankees had going for them,

beyond the roster of deeply talented players, was their immense experience. Some of their more confident sorts, like Derek Jeter, figured that once the playoffs began the Yankees would react instinctively, the way they had in '96 and '98 and '99, the way some of their newcomers—like David Justice—had for other playoff teams. They barely survived Oakland in the Division Series, and they lost Game 1 of the A.L. Championship Series to Seattle. Then there was a moment in Game 2 that Torre said he would remember forever, when the Yankees finally shed themselves of the slump, once and for all. The Yankees were trailing by 1–0 in the eighth inning, with Justice leading off, and a strike was called. Justice was furious and started to turn on the home plate umpire. But then Justice abruptly turned away and stepped out of the batter's box, as if it had just occurred

to him that there was no need—no time for him to get embroiled in a nasty argument. Battling the Seattle left-hander Arthur Rhodes, Justice whacked a double to left-center field. Bernie Williams had a great at-bat before lining a single over second to tie the score; suddenly, the entire Yankees' lineup had reverted to form, the hitters waiting patiently for pitches to hit, something they hadn't done in almost a month, and the Yankees scored seven runs that inning and outscored the Mariners by 31–15 from that point in the series.

Their confidence continued to grow, built on their experience. Clemens produced perhaps the greatest outing of his career against the Mariners in Game 4, striking out 15, allowing one hit. The Mets won the National League pennant Oct. 16, and the next day, the Yankees played Game 6, knowing they would

share in a Subway Series with a victory that night. Seattle led, 4–3, in the seventh inning, and Jose Vizcaino and Derek Jeter beat out infield hits. Justice came to bat, to face Rhodes, again—Justice, with more post-season at-bats than anyone in the history of baseball. He waited, checking his swing, working the count in his favor at 3 balls and 1 strike, and looked for a fastball, and got it. Some of the Yankees would speculate later that Justice's home run might have been the hardest ball they'd ever seen hit in Yankee Stadium, and veterans of Yankee Stadium were sure it was the first time they'd ever seen the different levels of the old ballpark rippling, under the stomping feet of fans. The same Yankees who hadn't been sure whether they should sip Champagne 19 days before were celebrating fervently now.

Roger Clemens (above, left) turned in one of the most dominant performances of his stellar career in A.L.C.S. Game 4; with the Mariners finally defeated, the Yankees (above) celebrated their return to the World Series for the third consecutive season.

# The Hard Way

By **BUSTER OLNEY**

The Yankees came out firing on all cylinders in Game 5, scoring six runs in the first inning, three of them on a double by Tino Martinez that drove in Derek Jeter (2), Paul O'Neill (crossing the plate) and David Justice; after the victory, even veteran Yankees like (left to right) Jeter, Scott Brosius and Luis Sojo were giddy with relief.

They were all tired and grumpy when their plane left Newark at about 12:30 a.m. Oct. 8, and the collective mood of the Yankees was not improved by their third cross-country flight in eight days. But they could only blame themselves. They stumbled into this three-of-five-game Division Series with Oakland, surrendering the home-field advantage with their late-season collapse, and in Game 1, the Athletics' extremely talented and young and inexperienced team had beaten them. Oakland scored three runs in the fifth inning to take a 3–2 lead over Roger Clemens, and after the Yankees tied the game in the top of the sixth, the light-hitting catcher Ramon Hernandez doubled home the go-ahead run off Clemens in the bottom of the inning and the Athletics won, 5–3.

Faced with the prospect of falling behind two games to none, the Yankees got a huge performance in Game 2 from Andy Pettitte, who threw seven and two-thirds shutout innings, but even then, there was some drama: the Yankees' offense was sputtering and they failed to score until the sixth inning, when they got a couple of fluke hits and managed three runs. Mariano Rivera relieved Pettitte, threw the final inning and a third, and with the series returning to Yankee Stadium for Games 3 and 4, the Yankees seemed in good shape once more.

Orlando Hernandez pitched Game 3 with far less than his best stuff and still contained the Athletics, causing them to strand five runners in the first four innings, and he generated a couple of double plays in his seven innings of work—remarkable, considering that he produced fewer double plays than almost any major league starting pitcher during the regular season. Luis Sojo scored one run and drove in an insurance run in the Yankees' 4–2 victory, and all they needed to finish off the Athletics in the series was for Clemens to close them out in Game 4, on Saturday, Oct. 7. The alternative was unthinkable: If Clemens and the Yankees lost Game 4, they would have to fly all the way across the country to play an elimination game. Which is precisely what occurred. Olmedo Saenz slammed a three-run homer off Clemens in the first inning of Game 4 and Oakland routed the Rocket, and while the Yankees slogged through an 11–1 loss—the Yankee Stadium fans watching listlessly and probably wondering if they were seeing the end of the dynasty—they had 3 hours 42 minutes to contemplate that terrible plane ride.

"There were a lot of angry people on that plane," Manager Joe Torre said afterward.

But any frustration or weariness they might have felt was unwittingly wiped away by a few flippant comments made by Oakland third baseman Eric Chavez a couple of hours before Game 5. Asked about the possibility that the Yankees' dominance might come to an end that night, Chavez, a gregarious sort who tries to accommodate reporters, responded with words in the past tense, suggesting that the Yankees' time had passed. What Chavez did not know was that his interview was being shown, live, on the giant twin scoreboards that loom over Network Associates Coliseum, and that the Yankees had heard every word as they began batting practice. "So, he's dropping the past tense on us, is he?" said Scott Brosius. "We'll see." Chuck Knoblauch, benched for Games 2, 3 and 4 and admonished by Torre for not working out, led off the game with a sharp single off Gil Heredia, and the Yankees kept pounding away, until they scored six runs in the first inning—their biggest rally in more than a month.

Oakland would not quit: The Athletics scored twice in the second inning and brought the tying run into the on-deck circle in the third, and by the fourth inning Pettitte had been knocked out, the lead was cut to 7–5 and the most seasoned Yankees players had begun counting the number of outs left in the game, like Little Leaguers might do. The Yankees still needed 16 outs when Mike Stanton relieved Pettitte in the fourth, and the set-up man got six of those remaining outs, striking out three, holding the lead, steadying the team, probably the single most critical pitching performance of the entire season. Jeff Nelson relieved Stanton in the sixth inning and got four outs, and El Duque came out of the bullpen for one out, his first post-season relief appearance. Rivera took over for the last five. When Chavez fouled out to end the game, the Yankees—most of whom had won three World Series—went berserk for about 10 to 15 minutes, shouting and hugging; Torre cried tears of relief. Getting past Oakland was so hard, he said. Nothing seemed to come easy for the Yankees in this season.

**Andy Pettitte (opposite, bottom) was dominant in Game 2, enabling the Yankees to tie the series at one game apiece; Luis Sojo (above) singled in a critical insurance run to ice Game 3; Olmedo Saenz (opposite, above) ripped a three-run homer off Roger Clemens in Oakland's Game 4 laugher, which forced the Yankees to return to the West Coast for the deciding contest.**

# Silenced by Seattle

Mark McLemore slid away from the tag of Yankees catcher Jorge Posada to score the game's first run in the fifth inning; Denny Neagle (opposite) looked disconsolate after Seattle's Alex Rodriguez (background) homered to give the Mariners a two-run lead in the sixth.

| LINE SCORE | | | | | | | | | | |
|---|---|---|---|---|---|---|---|---|---|---|
| **Seattle** | 0 | 0 | 0 | 0 | 1 | 1 | 0 | 0 | 0 | –2 |
| **New York** | 0 | 0 | 0 | 0 | 0 | 0 | 0 | 0 | 0 | –0 |

NEW YORK—Luis Sojo was due to bat for the Yankees in the ninth inning tonight, two outs, two runners on base, Seattle winning by two runs. And Yankees Manager Joe Torre had no intention of inserting a pinch-hitter for Sojo, a career utilityman, because two weeks into October, Sojo is the Yankees' most productive hitter.

The Yankees got by with that in the first round of the playoffs against Oakland. But now it is the second round, and Derek Jeter is not hitting, David Justice is not hitting, and Paul O'Neill is swinging so badly that he was removed for a pinch-hitter himself tonight.

Seattle's Freddy Garcia and the three relievers who followed him shackled the Yankees, 2-0, at Yankee Stadium in Game 1 of the American League Championship Series, except for the one brief moment in the ninth inning when it seemed Sojo might win the game.

But it is hard to know exactly if Garcia, who pitched exceptionally for six and two-thirds innings, was overwhelming, or if this was just the latest chapter in a Yankees slump that has lasted for about a month.

"I don't want to take any of the credit away from Garcia," Torre said, "but we have not been hitting the ball. We have not been scoring runs."

Long after last night's game ended, most of the Yankees were still hidden in unseen rooms in their clubhouse. The door to the trainer's

**Freddy Garcia (above) allowed just three hits in six and two-thirds innings, as his array of high-velocity pitches were all working; Glenallen Hill (above, middle) fanned in a key situation in the eighth.**

room, usually open, was closed, the players on the other side, alone with their meals and their thoughts.

Justice went 0 for 4, striking out twice. Jeter whiffed three times, looking as bad as he ever has in one game, swinging wildly. The Yankees compiled 6 hits and 13 strikeouts, and it would be easy to attribute this to Garcia and his brethren. "I'm not making any excuses for our guys," Torre said. "It is frustrating."

Denny Neagle started for the Yankees last night and gave them a chance to win. He talks as if his fast-forward button has jammed, words rushing out of his mouth rapidly; he spoke 1,050 words in answering the first six questions posed to him by the news media yesterday, or 932 more than Garcia used. Neagle's challenge tonight was in controlling that runaway energy, to work calmly.

Before the game, Torre said he would know very early how Neagle would pitch. Neagle was behind in the count constantly, but he battled, stayed in the game.

Neagle retired the first two batters in the fifth, his pitch count climbing toward 100, the score 0-0. But Mark McLemore pulled a line drive that bounced just inside the left-field line, a double. Rickey Henderson was next to bat and when the count reached two balls and two strikes, the Yankees' outfield coach, Lee Mazzilli, stood on the top step of the dugout and beckoned for right fielder Paul O'Neill to move in a few steps, waving his arms, trying desperately to get his attention.

O'Neill finally saw Mazzilli and moved toward the infield about 10 feet, just before Henderson singled to right. O'Neill was in a perfect position, shallow right field, to throw out McLemore. But his throw was off-line—like a number of his throws against Oakland in the division series—and Seattle had a 1-0 lead.

Alex Rodriguez opened the top of the sixth for the Mariners and again, Neagle worked into a deep pitch count, three balls and two strikes, and flipped a changeup to the outside corner. Rodriguez leaned over the plate, his weight shifted on his front foot, and bashed the ball; undoubtedly, it was going to go far enough to be a home run.

The only question was whether it would be

foul or fair, and it rippled the screen attached to the yellow foul pole, for a home run. Rodriguez and Jeter are close friends, but after the ball landed, Jeter turned his head and stared toward the third-base stands, and when Rodriguez passed on his jog around the bases, Jeter turned and looked to the other side of the field.

Jeter had already struck out twice by then, baffled, like many of his teammates, by Garcia. The right-handed Garcia, one of the little-known minor leaguers Seattle acquired from Houston a couple of years ago for Randy Johnson, missed most of this year with a leg injury. The Yankees had not seen him pitch this season, which was one of the reasons Seattle Manager Lou Piniella opted to pitch him in Game 1.

He was throwing hard, mixing his fastball with a curve, a slider, a forkball. "Everything," Jeter said. "He had everything."

O'Neill said: "When a guy throws that hard, you have to make a decision quick. He's got some kind of movement on the ball. I think we helped him by swinging at a lot of bad pitches."

The Yankees had runners at first and second and nobody out in the sixth, but Piniella chose to keep Garcia in the game, and he whiffed O'Neill and Bernie Williams, and retired Justice on a fly to deep center.

When Garcia's pitch count climbed over 100 in the seventh, Piniella went to his bullpen. The Yankees had a runner at first base and two out in the eighth, O'Neill was due to bat, and Torre replaced him with Glenallen Hill, looking for a home run that could tie the game. "You've got a guy with tremendous power on the bench," O'Neill said. "You've got to give your team a chance to tie up the game."

Hill whiffed, however, one of 22 strikeouts by the two teams, an A.L.C.S. record. Kazuhiro Sasaki relieved for Seattle in the ninth, and Williams and Martinez singled around Justice's strikeout. After Jorge Posada flied out, Sojo came to the plate; he led the Yankees with four runs batted in against Oakland.

With two strikes, Sojo popped a long fly down the right-field line, and he waved with his left hand, trying to guide the ball past the foul pole with body English. But it fell foul, to the right of the pole by 10 feet, and he then flied out to end the game.

**After retiring the Yankees' Luis Sojo to end the game, Seattle closer Kazuhiro Sasaki and catcher Joe Oliver celebrated the Mariners' victory.**

# Breaking Through

NEW YORK—The tension in the dugout was at high tide again, and Joe Torre tried a small joke. "Are you guys trying?" he asked Derek Jeter after the Yankees' streak of scoreless innings reached 20 today.

Yes, they were trying. Sometimes you are trying so hard that you squeeze the bat handle, Paul O'Neill explained, and the fans are yelling and reminding you that you need to try even harder. Soon you are so rigid that the act of hitting a baseball—something you have done since childhood—is like driving a stick shift for the first time, the gears grinding.

from inevitable defeat. The next three games of the series will be played in Seattle, and had there been a 2–0 deficit after two games, the Yankees' reign as World Series champions would have been in serious jeopardy.

"I just sense that we relieved a lot of pressure today," Torre said.

He said something along those lines after the Yankees clinched the division title despite being routed in Baltimore on Sept. 29, and after they won a playoff game five days later to snap an eight-game losing streak, and after they finally eliminated Oakland on Sunday.

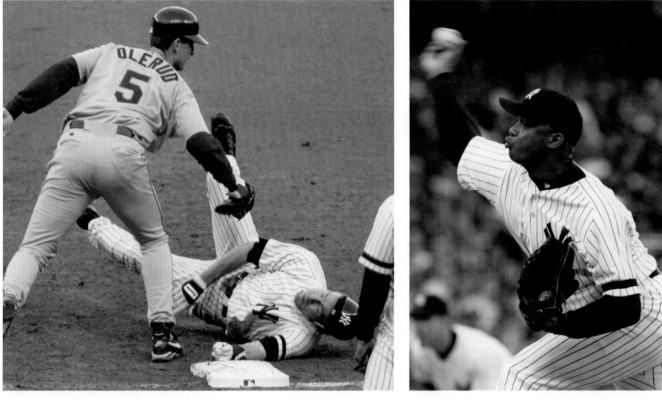

Yes, they were trying, losing by a run to Seattle in the eighth inning. But after Bernie Williams singled home the tying run in the bottom of the eighth, the Yankees finally relaxed and then exploded to beat the Mariners, 7–1, in Game 2 of the championship series.

Orlando Hernandez threw another masterly game, allowing one run in eight innings and improving his career postseason record to 7–0. The Yankees left Yankee Stadium last night feeling as if they had rescued themselves

The tension keeps rising and the Yankees have almost gone under several times, but they keep struggling, seemingly dog-paddling their way to the next game.

After Torre felt compelled to pinch-hit for the former All-Star O'Neill in Game 1, O'Neill poked his head inside Torre's office as he departed the Stadium. "Am I playing tomorrow?" O'Neill asked.

"Yeah, you're playing tomorrow," Torre replied forcefully.

Torre did adjust his lineup to account for O'Neill's slump, dropping him to seventh in the batting order, switching David Justice to third and Jorge Posada to sixth, and right

**In spite of ongoing frustrations like the pick-off of Scott Brosius in the third inning (above, left), Orlando Hernandez (above) kept the Yankees in the game until the New York bats exploded in the eighth, the most resounding shot being Derek Jeter's two-run homer (opposite) which put the contest out of reach.**

| LINE SCORE | | | | | | | | | | |
| --- | --- | --- | --- | --- | --- | --- | --- | --- | --- | --- |
| **Seattle** | 0 0 1 | | 0 0 0 | | 0 0 0 | | –1 |
| **New York** | 0 0 0 | | 0 0 0 | | 0 7 0 | | –7 |

**Manager Joe Torre (above), impassive as ever, had to breathe a sigh of relief after the Yankees offense awoke from its 21-inning slumber in the eighth inning; Luis Sojo (right) slid wildly across the plate with New York's fourth run of the game.**

away, the Yankees threatened. Chuck Knoblauch led off the first inning with a walk, and after Seattle second baseman Mark McLemore botched a potential double-play ball, John Halama, the Mariners' starter, walked Justice to load the bases.

But Williams, the Yankees' cleanup hitter, topped the ball two feet in front of the plate, and Seattle catcher Dan Wilson retrieved it, stepped on home and threw to first for a double play. Tino Martinez grounded out to end the inning without any runs, and the fans booed loudly, their heroes absorbing their frustration.

It got worse. Scott Brosius beat out an infield hit to open the third and was immediately picked off, falling awkwardly. The Yankees had runners on first and second and two out in the fifth, and Justice grounded out. They advanced another runner into scoring position with two out in the sixth but failed to score.

They were fortunate that Hernandez was

pitching. Seattle scored a run in the third on a two-out single by Stan Javier, but El Duque allowed only five other hits and struck out seven, at ease on the October stage.

When Martinez reached second with two outs in the sixth, O'Neill came to bat with the tying run in scoring position—and with only 13 hits in his last 82 at-bats. Fans in right field, for whom O'Neill has been an icon, rose, and the rest of the Yankees faithful followed, chanting his name.

O'Neill pulled a slow dribbler to the right side. He pumped his arms and legs, moving down the line in tight strides. First baseman John Olerud led Halama with the throw, and Halama and O'Neill both stomped on the bag at virtually the same instant. Out, signaled the umpire Wally Bell.

O'Neill slammed his helmet to the ground with both hands, turned and charged the umpire. "Sometimes you get caught

up in these games," O'Neill said later.

An inning later, the Yankees caught up to Seattle. After the Mariners' left-hander Arthur Rhodes took over for the Yankees eighth, his manager, Lou Piniella, decided not to make one other switch he thought about—replacing the defensively challenged Al Martin in left.

Justice led off for the Yankees. He smashed a high drive to left-center, the ball thumping high against the wall, maybe a foot or so from carrying over. It was a good start, and yet at the moment, it seemed like just another example of how the Yankees' offense was fated: so close to a home run, so close to tying the game.

Williams came to bat, looking to punch the ball to the right side and advance Justice to third. But Rhodes knew this and began jamming the right-handed-hitting Williams with fastballs. The count reached three and two, and Williams changed his approach. "I was like, 'Forget this, I'm just going to try to hit the ball any way I can,'" Williams said.

Rhodes spun a breaking ball and Williams fouled it off, barely, and fouled off two more pitches. On the eighth pitch of the at-bat,

Williams rifled a line drive toward second; Justice scored easily, and the top two decks of the old ballpark began quivering, the fans moving them.

The burden of tying the game was gone, and the Yankees relaxed. Martinez hit a liner to left, and off the bat, it appeared Martin would be able to make the catch easily. Martin hesitated, however, staggered forward, reached down, and the ball went in and out of his glove for a single.

The rest of the inning fell into place. Posada singled off McLemore's glove to score Williams with the go-ahead run; O'Neill hit a sacrifice fly, actually clapping his hands in relief; Luis Sojo singled; Jose Vizcaino doubled; Knoblauch singled; and Jeter slammed a homer, the hardest ball he has hit in a month and just the second Yankee homer in 88 innings.

The Yankees had not had a hit with runners in scoring position in 25 innings, and in the eighth inning yesterday, they had four in a row.

Are they trying? Yes. But they are resigned to the reality that nothing will come easy.

**David Justice ripped a long double off the wall to get the eighth-inning outburst under way.**

# Looking Like Themselves

Up against the wall: Seattle's Mike Cameron tumbled over the center-field fence (opposite) in a futile effort to catch a second-inning home run by Tino Martinez (right) that put the Yankees in front 2–1.

**LINE SCORE**

| | | | | | | | | | | | |
|---|---|---|---|---|---|---|---|---|---|---|---|
| **New York** | 0 | 2 | 1 | 0 | 0 | 1 | 0 | 0 | 4 | –8 |
| **Seattle** | 1 | 0 | 0 | 0 | 1 | 0 | 0 | 0 | 0 | –2 |

**SEATTLE**—The deeper the Yankees move into October, the more they look the way they usually do this time of year, confident and relaxed, on track, like the D train moving steadily through the Bronx.

The Yankees put a headlock on the Mariners tonight, when Bernie Williams and Tino Martinez ripped back-to-back homers among the team's 13 hits, Andy Pettitte pitched six and two-thirds solid innings and the bullpen closed out Seattle in an 8–2 victory. The Yankees hold a 2–1 advantage in the series.

Even if the Mariners rebound, they cannot win this series without winning at least one game in Yankee Stadium. "Tonight was the biggest game of the series," Yankees second baseman Luis Sojo said. "We need to get that one tomorrow, to make the series basically over."

Mariano Rivera relieved with one out in

**LEAGUE CHAMPIONSHIP SERIES 2000**

the eighth inning of a 4–2 game and a runner at second, and he retired the final five batters, extending his streak of consecutive scoreless innings in the postseason to 33⅓. That broke the 38-year-old record of the Yankees legend Whitey Ford (33 innings), set as a starter in the World Series from 1960 to 1962.

The Yankees scored seven runs in their final at-bat of Game 2, and Manager Joe Torre mentioned afterward that he noticed the patience in their at-bats, the approach that has become their trademark. "You probably couldn't have

mapped out a better game offensively for us," third baseman Scott Brosius said. "That's a great formula for us to win games."

And the Seattle starter, Aaron Sele, was probably the prototype pitcher for the Yankees to face when their offense is starting to emerge from its monthlong slump. Sele had 14 decisions in games with the Yankees and had lost 10 of them, including two playoff games while pitching for the Texas Rangers in 1998 and 1999. He was the Mariners' most consistent pitcher this year, winning 17 games dur-

**The beginning and the end: Bernie Williams (right) received congratulations after his second-inning solo home run opened the Yankee scoring; Mariano Rivera (above) was as unhittable as ever in his customary closer's role.**

ing the regular season and earning the trust of his manager. Lou Piniella aligned Sele as his Game 3 starter so that if the series were to extend to a Game 7, Sele would pitch that game as well.

But Sele carried to the mound all of that dubious history against the Yankees, and if that wasn't enough reason for self-doubt, there was this: In the early innings, Sele could not throw strikes with his curveball, the pitch with which he usually attacks hitters. He tried back-to-back curveballs to the leadoff hitter, Chuck Knoblauch, in the first inning and both bounced, and Sele struggled to make the correction in his release point, with some breaking balls spinning too high, some too far outside.

That made Sele vulnerable; the Yankees knew that when Sele had to throw a strike, he was going to throw a fastball, in all likelihood.

Williams led off the second inning after Seattle had scored a run in the bottom of the first. He got ahead in the count, 3-0, and looked for the sign from the third-base coach, Willie Randolph; it was a green light for

Williams to swing. When Sele threw a fastball thigh high, where Williams likes it, the Yankees' center fielder drove it five or six rows into the right-field stands.

Martinez followed, and got ahead in the count, 2-0; again, Sele had to throw a strike. The Seattle right-hander conceded a high fastball, and Martinez—the rarest of left-handed batters because he prefers high pitches to low pitches—hammered the ball to straightaway center field, over the wall, a monstrous homer. The Yankees hit two homers in their first 237 at-bats of the postseason, before Williams and Martinez went back to back and the Yankees had a 2-1 lead.

They added another run in the third. Derek Jeter was on first with two outs, David Justice at the plate, Williams on deck, and again Sele got into trouble. He went to 2-1 on Justice. Williams was looming on deck, his career average against Sele over .300, so Sele could not afford to walk Justice. He also

could not throw his curveball for a strike.

He threw to first, stepped off the rubber, seemingly reluctant to throw his next pitch. He needed to throw the fastball, as Justice had certainly ascertained, and Justice ripped a liner to left-center field, the ball shooting to the wall, Jeter sprinting around the bases with the Yankees' third run.

It wasn't until the middle innings that Sele finally began to throw his curveball for strikes. This is how predictable Sele was for the Yankees: They did not swing and miss until his 71st pitch, when Justice struck out in the sixth, and only that one time among his 90 pitches. "They spread it out and keep the pressure on you 1 to 9," Sele said. "They force you to make good pitch after good pitch, and I didn't do it."

Seattle sprayed nine hits against Pettitte, but he managed to limit the damage, getting Jay Buhner to ground out weakly and John Olerud to pop up to kill a rally in the first inning, breaking Rickey Henderson's bat in the second inning and producing a slow groundout with runners at second and third. The left-hander's resiliency bought time for his teammates to keep working on Sele.

Williams singled through the middle with one out in the sixth inning. Martinez chopped a dribbler up the first-base line, the ball rolling perhaps 40 feet. Sele darted over and picked up the grounder, but was unable to grip the ball and make a throw.

Jorge Posada flied deep to right field, enabling Williams to tag up and take third base and bringing Paul O'Neill to the plate. Sele fell behind, 2-0, in a defensive position again, and shortly thereafter O'Neill pulled a single through the hole between first and second to drive home Williams. It was O'Neill's first run-scoring hit since Sept. 23, after 15 unsuccessful attempts with runners in scoring position.

The Yankees kept pressing, tacking on four more runs in the ninth. Every starting position player other than Posada had at least one hit. Five players drove in runs, six scored runs.

The Yankees are gaining speed, with two more stops to go before the World Series.

Three men out: Seattle outfielders (left to right) Rickey Henderson, Mike Cameron and Stan Javier were understandably glum as they took a break during a ninth-inning pitching change.

# Roger, and Out

**Chin music: Roger Clemens (opposite) was dominant throughout his one-hit masterpiece, establishing early his willingness to pitch inside with a first-inning brushback of Alex Rodriguez (right).**

SEATTLE—Roger Clemens was trying to block out everything around him and focus on the Seattle Mariners tonight, but the information age is a tough place to hide when everybody in the ballpark and the baseball world is talking about you.

Clemens, the Yankee right-hander, saw all the zeroes on a television screen in the clubhouse after the fifth inning tonight and realized he had a no-hitter going. Clemens heard

broadcasters debating whether he purposely threw at Alex Rodriguez, the way many thought he had thrown at the Mets' Mike Piazza in July. He probably knew coming into the game that he had a reputation for failure in the postseason.

But Clemens ignored all that and, at 38, produced one of the greatest performances in playoff history, allowing one hit to the Seattle Mariners and striking out 15. With a 5-0 victory, the Yankees took a 3-1 lead in the championship series.

"It reminded me of Bob Gibson, the way he went out and hitched up his belt and went after hitters," Yankee Manager Joe Torre said.

Clemens's one-hitter was the first in League Championship Series history. He tied the L.C.S. record for strikeouts in a nine-inning game, set in 1997 by the Florida Marlins' Livan Hernandez. Gibson, pitching for the St. Louis Cardinals, set the record for most strikeouts in a postseason game when he struck out 17 Detroit Tigers in a World Series game in 1968.

"I feel real fortunate that I've been able to continue at this stage of my career," Clemens said, "to go out there and be a part of a great deal of excitement and have a chance to light it up. Sometimes you get beat, but tonight was special."

If Clemens has average stuff, his first fastball is often a two-seamer about 91 to 92 miles per hour, depending on how his legs feel, how loose he is. Tonight his first pitch was 96 m.p.h., and the message could not have been clearer if he had hung a 100-foot neon sign from the Space Needle: he felt extraordinary, a fact confirmed when he struck out the first two batters.

Then came the second part of Clemens's

| LINE SCORE | | | | |
|---|---|---|---|---|
| **New York** | 0 0 0 | 0 3 0 | 0 2 0 | −5 |
| **Seattle** | 0 0 0 | 0 0 0 | 0 0 0 | −0 |

**Blast-off: Two timely home runs—a three-run blast by Derek Jeter (above) in the fifth inning and a two-run shot by David Justice (right) in the eighth—produced all five Yankee runs.**

message, in code. Rodriguez batted with two out in the first inning and Clemens hurled a 97 m.p.h. fastball in the vicinity of his jaw. Rodriguez fell backward, spinning and staring out at Clemens, then at the Yankees' dugout, and then at Clemens again.

Clemens threw his next pitch in almost the same spot, making Rodriguez bend back again. It was Clemens's most overt brushback since he beaned Piazza on July 8.

The Mariners were incensed, Manager Lou Piniella turning and uttering obscenities to others in the dugout, Rodriguez staring at Clemens after he reached first base on a walk. "It's puzzling how that can happen when a guy has such good control," Rodriguez said later, after initially declining to comment several times. "He never misses up and away. He always misses up and in."

Jorge Posada, Clemens's catcher, batted with one out in the top of the second inning, and Paul Abbott, the Seattle starter, whipped a fastball over his head. Piniella rose off the Seattle bench and screamed in the direction of the Yankees' bench, to resolve any confusion Posada might have had over Abbott's intentions. "If he wants to throw at our guys, we'll throw at his guys, period," Piniella said.

Clemens said: "I've got no comment on that. I was trying to pitch A-Rod inside."

Before Clemens began warming up for the

bottom of the second, Umpire John Hirschbeck went to the mound, stood face to face with the pitcher and addressed him, presumably telling him that it might be a good idea if he did not respond to what Abbott had done. But Clemens had already achieved his purpose, and in the second inning he began finding his rhythm, mixing in more split-fingered fastballs, twice finishing off hitters with 98 m.p.h. fastballs.

Clemens retired the Mariners in order in the second inning, and the third. After there was one out in the fourth, Rodriguez fanned on a two-seam fastball, and Edgar Martinez grounded to shortstop.

Abbott was shutting out the Yankees, as well, but he had not pitched in nine days and was expected to last six innings at the most. Some of his fastballs began to sail at the outset of the fifth, a sign of weariness, and with two out, Scott Brosius poked a single through the

right side of the infield, Chuck Knoblauch walked and Jeter slammed a three-run homer.

Clemens was armed with a sizable lead and began establishing complete command of his breaking pitches, mixing his splitters and sliders. There were three weak outs in the fifth: a grounder to the pitcher, a strikeout and a popout to third, the last pitch of the inning clocking in at 98 m.p.h. Clemens had retired 13 consecutive batters and needed 12 more for a no-hitter, which would be the first of his career.

His first pitch to David Bell in the sixth inning registered at 99 m.p.h.; at the end of a 10-pitch at-bat, Bell popped out weakly to second. Clemens then cut down Dan Wilson and Stan Javier on strikes.

In the seventh, Clemens threw a fastball high to Al Martin, then tried a sinker down and in. Martin pulled a liner down the first-base line, and Clemens heard the ball tick off the top of Tino Martinez's outstretched glove and down into the right-field corner for a double. The no-hitter was over. "I couldn't catch it," Martinez said later. "It's not like I could've done something differently and caught it."

Clemens had to refocus: Rodriguez and Edgar Martinez were due to bat, and between them they had the potential of propelling Seattle back into the game. Clemens's pitch count had exceeded 100, and with two relievers warming up in the Yankees' bullpen, he might have sensed he was close to being relieved. Bearing down, he struck out Rodriguez swinging and Martinez looking.

John Olerud walked, but Clemens zipped a fastball over the outside corner to fan Mike Cameron, and pumped his right fist. He struck out two more in the eighth and two more in the ninth, and when the game was over, Torre held his right hand on the side of Clemens's head. "That was special, Roger," he said, and smiled. "That was absolutely dominant."

# Leaving the Door Open

Five in the fifth: John Olerud (right) followed Alex Rodriguez's two-run single and Edgar Martinez's two-run homer with a solo shot of his own to put the Mariners in front by the final margin of 6–2.

| LINE SCORE | | | | |
|---|---|---|---|---|
| New York | 0 0 0 | 2 0 0 | 0 0 0 | –2 |
| Seattle | 1 0 0 | 0 5 0 | 0 0 x | –6 |

SEATTLE—Roger Clemens knocked the Mariners off their feet in October's tug of war in Game 4 yesterday, and when Luis Sojo ripped a two-run double early in Game 5 this afternoon, he could feel Seattle tumbling and collapsing once and for all. One big hit; that's all that was needed to finish the job.

But the finishing blow never came today, and Seattle regained its footing in the American League Championship Series, coming back to beat the Yankees, 6–2, when reliever Jeff Nelson surrendered three consecutive hits in the fifth inning: a two-run single by Alex Rodriguez and back-to-back homers by Edgar Martinez and John Olerud.

The Yankees are still in excellent position to eliminate the Mariners, leading the series, 3-2. But they could have closed out Seattle here. They could have opened the 15 cases of Champagne and enjoyed a cheery flight home before having a week of off-days and workouts before the World Series.

Now it is more complicated than that; there is work to be done. George Steinbrenner, the team's principal owner, walked out of the clubhouse sternly. "See you in New York," he said.

Sojo said: "We blew it. We had the bases loaded, I hit that double, and we didn't score after that. I thought we had it."

The Mariners might have thought so, too. They mustered only five runs in the first four games, and Clemens made them look like Little League rejects in his one-hitter in Game 4.

It was dreary and damp and cold today, and Seattle Manager Lou Piniella might have sensed the gloom in his team, screaming about an inside pitch to Martinez in the first inning that seemed harmless.

But the Yankees' starter, Denny Neagle, was tedious in his caution today, pitching as if he did not want to risk any contact by the Mariners; later he said that he felt he had made a lot of good pitches, that he pitched better than the results indicated.

Neagle reached three-ball counts against 7 of the first 13 batters he faced. He walked

Freddy Garcia (above) struggled, allowing seven hits in five innings, but he avoided major damage and in the end it was Alex Rodriguez (right, circling the bases on Edgar Martinez's home run in the fifth) and the Mariners who survived to play another day.

Mike Cameron, Rodriguez and Martinez in order in the first inning and got away with allowing just one run, but threw 30 pitches. The circumstances seemed to control him, and the count often favored the Seattle hitters.

The Mariners' Freddy Garcia had a similar outing. He was in trouble early, but the big, fatal hit eluded the Yankees, who had runners on base in each of the first three innings and could not score.

The Yankees loaded the bases with nobody out in the fourth inning, and Sojo slammed a two-run double to give them a 2-1 lead. They could sense that one more big hit was all that was needed.

But Scott Brosius, who stranded two runners in the second inning, popped up for the first out, Chuck Knoblauch struck out and Derek Jeter grounded out.

The Yankees had a runner at second and one out in the fifth, and that did not produce any runs. The game was there for the taking

and the Yankees passed. "We had a chance to put them away early in the game," Jeter said, "and we didn't do it."

Mark McLemore led off the Seattle fifth with a bunt single on the third-base side. When the left-handed Neagle fell behind in the count to Rickey Henderson, Nelson started throwing in the bullpen.

Nelson usually pitches in the seventh and eighth innings. But with the Yankees ahead by 2-1, both teams scheduled for a day off on Monday and three consecutive right-handed hitters set to follow Henderson, Yankees Manager Joe Torre was going for the kill. If Neagle could come back to close out the inning, or if Nelson could shut down the Mariners, then the Yankees would be four innings removed from their 37th pennant.

Neagle walked Henderson, however, giving the Mariners first and second and nobody out. After both runners advanced on Cameron's sacrifice bunt, Torre summoned Nelson, and

Neagle's shoulders sagged visibly; the reality is that he has not engendered the full measure of Torre's trust. "The competitive side of me would love to stay in," Neagle said, "but that's not my call."

Torre has relied heavily on Nelson in the postseason in his five years as the team's manager, and with Rodriguez and Martinez coming to bat, Torre was looking for Nelson to contain the damage. But Nelson did not feel right; his fastball had been sluggish as he warmed up, and he thought he was pitching with less than his best.

Rodriguez—5 for 12 in previous at-bats against Nelson—lined a single to left field for two runs, pushing Seattle to a 3–2 lead and revitalizing the Safeco Field fans.

Rodriguez took a lead off first base with one out. He had stolen a base effortlessly in Game 3 with Nelson on the mound, taking advantage of the right-hander's deliberate windup, and now Nelson worked hard to try to hold Rodriguez at first. Nelson threw to first five times and shortened his stride to the plate.

Nelson, however, was creating a problem for himself, falling behind Martinez, 2-0. Martinez saw all of this and took it in. With the situation and the count in his favor, Martinez looked for a fastball, and when Nelson threw a 91-mile-per-hour fastball, Martinez crushed a two-run homer to straightaway center field. The Mariners led, 5-2.

Nelson looked on impassively as Martinez rounded the bases, but his first fastball to Olerud was only 89 m.p.h., the diminished velocity a sign of discouragement: Olerud, too, slugged a home run to center field.

Nelson allowed two homers during the regular season and surrendered back-to-back shots in the fifth inning today; two of the four homers he has allowed this year were hit by Martinez. "I just made some bad pitches and it cost me," he said.

There were a few failed rallies late in the game. Glenallen Hill struck out while pinch-hitting for Paul O'Neill with the bases loaded and two out in the seventh. But the Yankees had botched the game before that when they could not score. The Mariners will go on for at least one more game.

**Jeff Nelson (above, being removed from the game by Joe Torre in the fifth) did not have his good stuff, allowing a single and a pair of home runs to the three batters he faced.**

# Next Stop: Subway Series

Two toward the title: A double by Jorge Posada (right) in the fourth inning produced two runs en route to the Yankee victory and yet another celebration of a World Series berth (opposite).

| LINE SCORE | | | | | | | | | |
|---|---|---|---|---|---|---|---|---|---|
| Seattle | 2 0 0 | | 2 0 0 | | 0 3 0 | | –7 |
| New York | 0 0 0 | | 3 0 0 | | 6 0 x | | –9 |

**NEW YORK**—The hopes and fears of New York baseball fans are a reality.

The Yankees will play the Mets in the city's first Subway Series since 1956, and the first ever between these two franchises, after the Yankees' wild pennant-clinching victory at Yankee Stadium early this morning.

With the Yankees trailing Seattle by 4-3 in the seventh inning, David Justice—one of the team's many important additions during the regular season—rocketed a three-run homer into the right-field stands for a 6–4 New York lead. Moments after the ball disappeared and the fans beckoned Justice for a curtain call, they began a chant: "We want the Mets!"

The Yankees added three more runs in the inning, and needed them all to hold off the Mariners in a 9–7 victory in Game 6 of the American League Championship Series. Now they will try to become the first team since the 1972-74 Athletics to win three straight World Series titles.

For six innings last night, it seemed the Yankees might be in jeopardy of being pushed to a Game 7 with the Mariners—and perhaps out of the playoffs. Seattle took a 4–0 lead in

the fourth inning against the Yankees' Orlando Hernandez, a stunning development, for El Duque had never lost in the postseason.

The Yankees pieced together a three-run rally in the bottom of the fourth, and for the next two and a half innings the two teams fended off rallies, Seattle's one-run advantage holding. Jose Paniagua took over in relief for Seattle in the seventh, and Jose Vizcaino was inserted as a pinch-hitter for Scott Brosius to lead off the inning for the Yankees.

Vizcaino topped a slow roller to the right

**Slick fielding by Tino Martinez (spearing a sharp grounder from Stan Javier in the third inning) and a mammoth three-run blast by David Justice (opposite) helped cement the victory.**

side of the infield, just out of the reach of first baseman John Olerud. Second baseman Mark McLemore gloved the ball and threw too late to Paniagua covering the bag.

Vizcaino was the potential tying run and Chuck Knoblauch bunted him to second. Derek Jeter dribbled a grounder to the left side, the ball trickling between the shortstop and third baseman; Vizcaino, unsure of whether to stay at second or advance, rambled to third.

With the left-handed-hitting Justice coming to bat, Seattle Manager Lou Piniella called for the left-hander Arthur Rhodes. When this series started, Justice had three hits in eight career at-bats against Rhodes, a hard thrower, and in Game 2 Rhodes allowed a double to Justice to start a seven-run rally.

Now it was Game 6, tying run at third, potential lead run at first. Justice stepped into

the box, hoping to hit a sacrifice fly, "to do anything to get that runner home from third. You got a guy there throwing 95 miles per hour, and I just didn't want to chase anything high. I've been having a problem doing that."

Justice took two pitches out of the strike zone, fouled off a pitch. Two balls and one strike. Rhodes fired a pitch that darted out of the strike zone and Justice tried to check his swing—successfully, according to the third-base umpire, Mark Hirschbeck, who flattened his hands to signal safe, a call that drew screams from Piniella. It was pivotal, for now the count was 3-1 and Justice could confidently look for a fastball.

He was calm in this situation; Justice has played in more games in the postseason than any other player in baseball history: 88. "He's lived in the postseason," Jeter said recently.

Rhodes threw a fastball. Justice lifted his right foot, and it darted forward, like a cobra's head, his bat following. He absolutely killed the ball, the sound of contact unmistakable. He knew he had hit a home run.

Jeter raised both arms, and several Yankees jumped from the dugout, the fans standing and jumping, the stands shaking. Justice turned toward first base and pumped his left arm, and afterward, he was near tears as he described how he looked into the stands rounding second base and saw fans going crazy. "I wish you all could have experienced that feeling," he said, gulping.

Soon there was the chant—"We want the Mets!"—and the Yankees pounded away at Rhodes for three more runs, Paul O'Neill driving in the last two with a single, runs that seemed like chips and soda for the party.

The Yankees led, 9–4, and were in full control.

But nothing has been easy for this team, and it would not be a simple matter of getting the last six outs. Alex Rodriguez slammed a homer leading off the eighth to knock out El Duque, and even when Mariano Rivera came on, bearing his three-year postseason scoreless streak, the Mariners continued to cut into the Yankees' lead. McLemore ripped a two-run double, ending Rivera's record streak at 33⅓ innings. Yankees 9, Mariners 7, three outs to go.

The one player who has hit Rivera harder than any other is Edgar Martinez, the Seattle

designated hitter, who came into this series with 10 hits in 12 at-bats against him. Torre had tried to maneuver around that matchup, but as he waited for the ninth inning, he and the bench coach Don Zimmer agreed that inevitably, Martinez would probably bat against Rivera in the ninth.

Martinez was due to bat fourth in the inning, and Rivera retired the first two batters. But Rodriguez beat out an infield single and Martinez walked to the plate, the potential tying run.

Rivera threw a fastball and Martinez hit a dribbler toward shortstop, where Jeter rushed in and threw to first, and when Tino Martinez caught the ball with his foot on the bag, Jeter leaped into the air. Catcher Jorge Posada hugged Rivera, Jeter ran up and body-slammed Rivera from behind; they were

American League champions again.

Torre walked onto the field and the first player he saw was Rivera, who grinned at his manager, having put him through an emotional wringer in those last two innings. "I knew it was going to come down to Martinez," said Torre, smiling.

They sprayed Champagne, 15 cases of Moet, and hugged. They will enjoy this for a day, then focus on the Mets, their tough little brother franchise across the city, a resilient team they have faced during the regular season. A month ago, Paul O'Neill shook his head at the thought the Yankees might play the Mets in the World Series. "I just couldn't handle that," he said. "I just couldn't handle that. It would just be too much."

But now it's reality, the fulfillment of the hopes and fears of players and fans alike.

The World Series

# Yankee Know-How

**By BUSTER OLNEY**

Already a veteran of 14 World Series games, the sage Yankee chuckled when, on the eve of the first Subway Series in 44 years, he was told that the Mets left fielder Benny Agbayani had told Howard Stern and Regis that the Mets would win in five games. It takes courage to do something like that, Derek Jeter said, his laughter born of experience. Never mind that Jeter is 26 years old and Agbayani is 28: On the World Series stage, the Yankees were the sage old-timers, familiar with the pitfalls and trappings, and the Mets were the talented understudies, sure of themselves even as they were gawking at the window dressings. One Yankee official said he knew the Mets would lose three hours before Game 1 of the World Series: When the Met team bus arrived at Yankee Stadium, the first two players who stepped off were holding cameras, as they videotaped the event for posterity.

Paul O'Neill began the World Series with four championship rings, as did David Cone. David Justice had one, Bernie Williams three, Jeter three, Mike Stanton three. Orlando Hernandez defected from Cuba less than three years ago and yet he already had as many

Derek Jeter's opening salvo (opposite) in Game 4 put the Yankees in front early en route to their 3–2 victory; in the ninth inning of Game 1, Paul O'Neill battled through a tough at-bat to draw a walk against Armando Benitez, then trotted home with the tying run three hitters later (left).

inches thick. What the Yankees' scouts believed before the series began is that the Mets hitters were all glaringly vulnerable, if the Yankees' pitchers could execute properly. Timo Perez had been a star in the first two rounds of the playoffs, but he had only one walk in 41 plate appearances and the Yankees were sure that he would chase high fastballs. Same with Jay Payton, and even Mike Piazza, the All-Star catcher, so long as the pitches were thrown in a proper sequence. Edgardo Alfonzo would swing at breaking balls low and away.

But even with the reports, the Yankees found themselves trailing 3–2 in the bottom of the ninth inning of Game 1. The Mets' inexperience had manifested itself earlier, when Perez assumed Todd Zeile's long fly ball in the sixth inning was going to be a home run and was subsequently thrown out at the plate when the drive hit the top of the wall. Paul O'Neill came to the plate with one out in the ninth inning, facing the hard-throwing closer Armando Benitez; in the previous month, the 37-year-old O'Neill looked 57 and had trouble with just about anyone throwing anything, and he was totally overmatched against Benitez. But O'Neill determined merely to survive in his at-bat, fouling off four pitches to the left side with two strikes and hanging on until he could finally coax a walk. Luis Polonia lined a single and Jose Vizcaino singled, and O'Neill eventually scored the tying run on a sacrifice fly. The Yankees would win in 12 innings, and when it was all over—when the series was over—O'Neill's at-bat was seen as the pivotal moment, when the experience and gritty nature of the Yankees had prevailed. O'Neill would bat .474 in the series.

The Mets had other chances, of course, winning Game 3 and going into Game 4 with hopes of tying the series. But Jeter, the sage shortstop, bashed a home run on the game's first pitch and everything turned again. By the fourth game, the Mets' hitters were swinging wildly, anxiously; during the Subway Series, they would draw 11 walks and accumulate 48

rings as any Met player, and two more than almost all of them. Roger Clemens came to the Yankees with an unfair reputation for big-game blowups, but in his last start in the American League playoffs, he had struck out 15 and allowed one hit—and besides, he had pitched in two World Series. No, Jeter would not make any predictions, because he'd learned to sidestep post-season time bombs like that. If Jeter had said what was on his mind, these might have been his words: Of course we will win. We are the champions, we have been here before, and the Mets will have to take the series from us; we will concede nothing. The Yankee players believed this.

They believed in their experience, in their ability to rise to the occasion, in their preparation. Separate groups of Yankee players met for more than an hour with the team's scouting staff the day before the start of the series, to discuss the detailed reports on the Mets, contained within black binders about 1½

Four days after the game- and Series-clinching hit from Luis Sojo in Game 5 (opposite), the happy Yankees, including Derek Jeter (above, middle) and (below, left to right) Denny Neagle, Paul O'Neill and Andy Pettitte, were basking in the adulation of the delirious throngs who flocked to lower Manhattan for the celebratory parade.

strikeouts, while the Yankees' hitters drew 25 walks and had 40 strikeouts.

Luis Sojo, a utilityman with three championship rings, drove home the winning run in the ninth inning of Game 5, and four days later, the Yankees were dodging rolls of toilet paper and strips of confetti again, in their fourth parade to City Hall in five years. Joe Torre, the Yankees' manager, called for O'Neill and David Cone to speak last, knowing that the core of the team may well change before the 2001 season. But Jeter and Bernie Williams and Mariano Rivera and other long-time Yankees will come back to try for a fourth straight title, battle tested, making no predictions on how long the dynasty will last, setting no limits.

**October 21, 2000 / Yankees 4 / Mets 3**

# One Long Night

Andy Pettitte (left) pitched effectively for the Yankees but left the game after seven innings on the losing end of a 3–2 score; five innings later Jose Vizcaino (opposite), a former Met, drove home the winning run.

| LINE SCORE | | | | |
|---|---|---|---|---|
| Mets | 0 0 0 | 0 0 0 | 3 0 0 | 0 0 0 | –3 |
| Yankees | 0 0 0 | 0 0 2 | 0 0 1 | 0 0 1 | –4 |

THE BRONX—It was the first Subway Series contest in 44 years, and the Yankees and the Mets played a game at Yankee Stadium that seemed to last almost that long, a night and an early morning of extra innings and base-running mistakes, heart-pounding comebacks and blown rallies.

But the longest game in terms of time in World Series history finally ended this morning after 4 hours 51 minutes, when Jose Vizcaino—the 101st batter of the game—singled

home Tino Martinez with two outs and the bases loaded in the bottom of the 12th. Martinez crossed the plate at 1:04 a.m., giving the Yankees a 4–3 victory.

The Yankees, who tied this Game 1 in the bottom of the ninth when they scraped out a run against the Mets' closer, Armando Benitez, have won a record 13 consecutive World Series games.

"We came with very little World Series experience, and we got a lot of it in one night," said Bobby Valentine, the Mets' manager.

The Mets came within two outs of winning, of seizing the advantage early in this series. The left-hander Al Leiter pitched excep-

Costly error: Timo Perez was thrown out at home in the sixth inning after slowing down while rounding the bases, certain that a ball hit by Todd Zeile had left the ballpark.

tionally for seven innings. The Mets had scored three runs in the top of the seventh, two on a single by the pinch-hitter Bubba Trammell, after the Yankees scored two in the bottom of the sixth. It looked as if the Mets were going to overcome a base-running blunder by Timo Perez, who was thrown out at the plate for the final out of the sixth inning after slowing down on the bases because he thought Todd Zeile's smash to left field was going to be a home run. Zeile's ball hit the top of the wall and stayed in play, and the Mets got nothing for it.

Benitez strolled to the mound for the bottom of the ninth, 6 feet 4 inches and 250 pounds, a huge presence making his World Series debut.

Paul O'Neill came to bat with one out, his bat speed slowed at age 37, and he fought to keep up with Benitez's fastball. O'Neill fouled off one pitch after another, always to the left side of the field with defensive swings, and slowly, the ball-strike count turned in his favor. On the 10th pitch of the at-bat, O'Neill drew a walk. Valentine later deflected questions about Benitez's control by crediting O'Neill: "He did a good job of hitting."

Joe Torre, the Yankees' manager, agreed: "It was amazing, really."

Scott Brosius was due to bat, but Luis Polonia was inserted as a pinch-hitter. On Friday, Polonia sat at his locker and talked about this very situation. He knew he was going to face Benitez, he said. Polonia faced Benitez for years

in winter ball in the Dominican Republic, and he felt that he knew how Benitez thinks. Polonia rifled a single to right field. Vizcaino was due to hit, and Torre eschewed the possible pinch-hitters Jose Canseco and Glenallen Hill because he wanted someone who had a better chance of putting the ball in play.

Vizcaino slapped a single to left, the crowd roaring when the ball landed. O'Neill pulled into third and stopped, leaving the bases loaded, one out. Under duress, the Yankees were reverting to form, taking at-bats pitch to pitch.

Chuck Knoblauch smashed a high fly ball to left field, where Joe McEwing retreated. But as soon as the ball went in the air, the 55,913 fans realized it was deep enough for O'Neill to tag up and score.

But the winning run would elude the Yankees repeatedly. They had runners at second and third and nobody out in the bottom of the 10th, the winning run only 90 feet from home. The Mets' infielders and outfielders moved in, and when Martinez looped a ball into shallow left field, McEwing rushed in and caught the pop only 20 feet or so from the infield for the first out of the inning.

The Mets left-hander Glendon Rusch, who was inserted into the game after Dennis Cook issued two walks to start the inning, intentionally walked Jorge Posada to fill the bases and create a force at every base. Mets fans were chanting, Yankees fans answering.

O'Neill chopped a grounder up the middle, and second baseman Edgardo Alfonzo fielded

**Todd Zeile was as certain as Timo Perez that his sixth-inning fly ball went into the stands before bouncing back into the field of play; his outrage (above) at the umpire's call notwithstanding, the ball actually landed on the top of the wall.**

David Justice drove in the first two runs of the World Series with a double in the sixth inning that scored Chuck Knoblauch and Derek Jeter.

the ball and flipped to second to start an inning-ending double play that sucked the air from the lungs of Yankees fans. The Mets had a reprieve, and several came spilling from the dugout to greet Rusch and his fielders.

The Yankees threatened again in the 11th, putting runners at second and third with two outs. But the pinch-hitting Hill popped up against Mets reliever Turk Wendell, Yankees fans groaning again. It was past midnight; the game that started on Oct. 21 would end Oct. 22.

The Yankees' bullpen had pinned down the Mets, Mariano Rivera pitching the 9th and 10th innings, Mike Stanton shutting them out in the 11th and 12th.

Martinez, who flubbed one chance in the 10th, singled off Wendell with one out in the

12th. Posada then smashed a liner past Alfonzo, the ball rolling against the grain of the defense, going between the outfielders for a double, Martinez stopping at third.

O'Neill was intentionally walked, the infielders and outfielders moved in, and Luis Sojo fouled out. There were two outs, and Vizcaino was next.

He had been a spare-part acquisition by the Yankees in June, acquired after Knoblauch's throwing problems had gone into full bloom. Brian Cashman, the Yankees general manager, traded the veteran Jim Leyritz for him, and Vizcaino played regularly for the next six weeks.

But when the Yankees signed Sojo in August, Vizcaino's playing time was reduced to almost nothing. Sojo started every game at

A two-run single by Bubba Trammell (left) and an infield hit beaten out by Edgardo Alfonzo (below) produced the three runs that put the Mets in front in the seventh inning.

second base in the first two rounds of the playoffs, and when Torre announced that Vizcaino would start in Game 1 of the World Series, it was a surprise. Torre picked him because of his .526 career average against Leiter, the Mets' starter.

But as the game progressed, Torre had decided against pinch-hitting for him a couple of times, and now Vizcaino was batting in the 12th inning, the winning run 90 feet away, against Wendell.

"I was really very comfortable," Vizcaino said. "I was just looking to put the ball in play."

Wendell threw a fastball outside, the 396th pitch of the game, trying to get ahead in the count, and Vizcaino—batting left-handed—sprayed the ball to the opposite field. There was no question, once it left his bat, that he had just won the game.

The fans rose, exploded, and as Martinez raced down the third-base line, Vizcaino leapt into the air once, pumped a fist, hit first base. Derek Jeter was among the first to reach him, hugging him, and others followed, pounding him on the back after the longest Series game since the Yankees and the Atlanta Braves needed 4:17 to play Game 4 in 1996.

"If Viz didn't get that hit," Jeter said in the jubilant Yankees' clubhouse, "we'd probably be out there another couple of hours."

Valentine seemed tense at the postgame news conference, tapping an index finger, and understandably. The Mets came so close to getting ahead, but now they are in the same position as the '98 Padres and the '99 Braves, trying to hold back champions who have proven to be so tough in October.

# Going Batty

Clemens' bizarre decision to hurl the shard of broken bat (opposite) toward Mike Piazza nearly provoked a brawl as the benches cleared and players from both teams massed near the pitcher's mound (right).

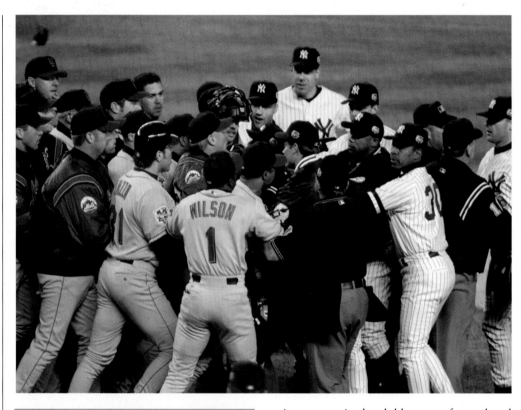

| LINE SCORE | | | | |
|---|---|---|---|---|
| Mets | 0 0 0 | 0 0 0 | 0 0 5 | –5 |
| Yankees | 2 1 0 | 0 1 0 | 1 1 x | –6 |

THE BRONX—Roger Clemens threw fastballs that reached 99 miles an hour, but drew even more attention for firing a broken bat in the direction of the Mets' Mike Piazza tonight, pitching eight shutout innings and heightening the emotions of the Subway Series that is being controlled by the Yankees.

Facing Piazza for the first time since hitting the Mets catcher in the head with a fastball in July, Clemens sparked an astonishing bench-clearing incident in the first inning by hurling the broken bat. But Clemens retreated to a private room in the clubhouse, refocused and continued his recent postseason domination, allowing only two hits and striking out nine in a 6–5 victory over the Mets in Game 2 of the World Series at Yankee Stadium. The Mets rallied to score all their runs in the last inning. Now the Yankees have won when facing the Mets' two best pitchers—Al Leiter was their Game 1 starter—and lead the Series by 2–0, extending their record streak of World Series victories to 14.

Clemens shut out Seattle on one hit in Game 4 of the American League Championship Series eight days ago, and in his last two games, opposing hitters are 3 for 55 (.055) against him, with 24 strikeouts.

Derek Jeter (above, fore-ground) signaled the out after David Justice made a sliding catch on a Mike Piazza line drive in the sixth inning; Mike Hampton (middle, foreground) looked heavenward as Tino Martinez lined a double up the alley in right-center field to drive in the Yankees' fourth run in the fifth inning.

But Clemens and his manager, Joe Torre, became animated when questioned after the game about Clemens's intent when he threw the bat at Piazza. "There was no intent there," Clemens said repeatedly.

Torre said: "It was just emotional. Should he have done it? No."

Clemens's beaning of Piazza three and a half months ago has hovered over this Series, and although Torre has accused the news media of reopening the wound in the last week, the Mets' hostility toward Clemens has never really dissipated. Everything Clemens did last night would be seen by the Mets through the prism of that incident in July.

Some of the Yankees had been concerned about Clemens's mood after a week in which the beaning was revisited time and again, and some

of them tried to pump him up during the day. Clemens wore linebacker's eyes to the mound. He wears a mouthpiece when he pitches, and his lower jaw was locked, his chin pushed forward, except when he cursed, either at himself or the batter, or at no one in particular.

Timo Perez faked a bunt on Clemens's first pitch and Clemens breathed two words, one syllable apiece: verbal aggression. He shook his head between pitches, talked aloud, his inner frenzy and his fastball both gaining speed. He struck out Perez with fastballs, all of them 97 m.p.h., and twice he threw 98-m.p.h. fastballs to Edgardo Alfonzo, before finishing off the second baseman with a 94-m.p.h. split-ter—a stunning speed for that diving pitch.

Piazza was announced as the next hitter and the crowd of 56,059 roared, the culmina-

tion of 106 days of anticipation for the first confrontation between the two men since Clemens beaned Piazza on July 8. The pitcher pumped two fastballs for strikes. Then, after throwing a ball out of the strike zone, Clemens fired inside, shattering Piazza's bat into at least three pieces.

The ball went foul and the barrel of the bat bounced toward Clemens, who fielded it as he would a grounder, then turned and fired the fragment sidearm toward Piazza, the bat head skimming and skittering along the ground just in front of Piazza.

Piazza was stunned, and he turned and stared at Clemens, moving toward the pitcher, turning the bat handle in his hand, stepping across the base line. The Mets coaching staff and players immediately rushed from their dugout. Clemens held his hand up, as if to ask the umpire for a new ball, but then came face to face with Piazza, appearing to tell Piazza that he thought the barrel was the ball.

Piazza said in July that he had lost respect for Clemens, and having just seen a bat go flying across his path, Piazza was stunned. He shouted at Clemens, asking him what his problem was. Then the Mets' bench coach, John Stearns—who had tried to confront Clemens the day after the beaning—bulled his way toward the pitcher, screaming. The two hordes of Yankees and Mets were bunched together, some pushing, the group turning slowly, like a satellite image of a hurricane.

Torre grabbed Stearns, who used to play for him, and tried to calm him down, and gradually, as Clemens and Piazza were sepa-

**Scott Brosius, mired in an agonizing late-season slump, launched a home run over the left-field wall in the second inning; the run batted in was only his second since Sept. 10.**

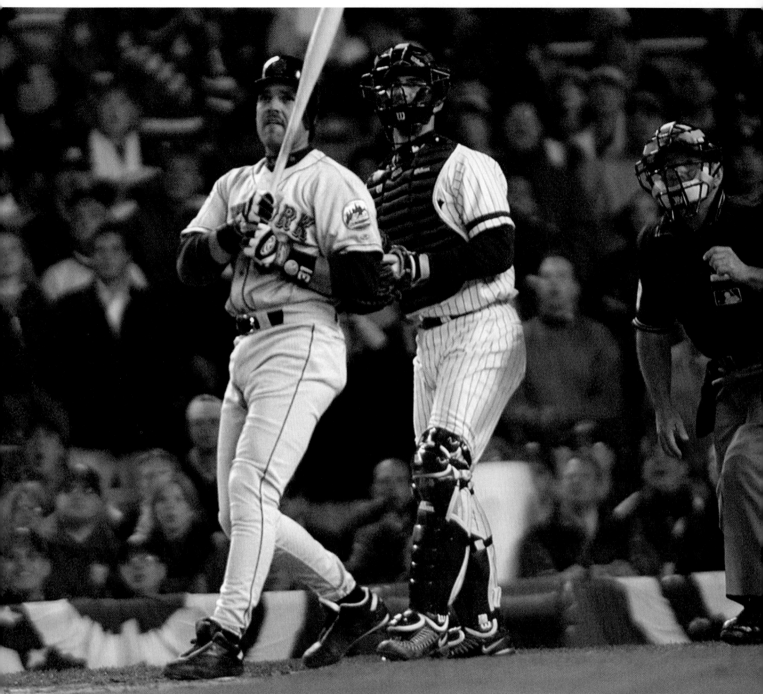

rated, the situation came under control with-out punches. But in his moment of anger or mania, Clemens heated those simmering emo-tions back to a full boil, by throwing a bat head and not a baseball. It felt surreal. After Piazza grounded out to second, the crowd was still murmuring while Clemens stopped and talked to the plate umpire, Charlie Reliford, explaining his actions.

What he told Reliford was close to what he said after the game—that he had thrown the bat without knowing where Piazza was, and when he looked up, he was surprised to see Piazza standing where he had thrown the bat. "I had no idea that Mike was running," Clemens said. "No idea."

Piazza was unsure, even after the game, about what happened, calling it bizarre. For an inning afterward, Mets Manager Bobby Valentine asked his players what had hap-pened, because he hadn't seen Clemens throw the bat. There was no consensus, Valentine said, among his players, and Valentine said that if he had seen the incident, he might have handled it differently, asking the umpires for clarification on whether Clemens should have been ejected.

But Valentine added: "I didn't see one hitter who was intimidated. I hate to tip my hat to the guy with the good stuff, but he had great stuff tonight."

And Mike Hampton, the Mets' pitcher, struggled. Everybody was on edge now, and it wasn't as if Hampton, the Mets' high-strung starter, needed any more emotions. Hampton finished off the National League Championship Series with a remarkable performance against the St. Louis Cardinals, and in the first inning of his first World Series appearance, he lost touch with the strike zone.

He retired the first two batters and then walked David Justice on four pitches. He walked Bernie Williams on four more. Hampton threw another ball to Tino Martinez, and the Mets' pitching coach, Dave Wallace, went to the mound to settle Hampton.

But Martinez lined a single to left, and Justice scored. Jorge Posada followed with a single on a 3–2 pitch—one of 32 pitches Hampton threw in the inning—and Williams scored. Rick White got up and started throwing in the Mets' bullpen.

Hampton got out of the inning trailing, 2–0, but Scott Brosius homered to lead off the second inning, his first home run since Sept. 10, and only his second run batted in since then. Hampton continued to struggle, rushing his delivery, and Jose Vizcaino reached first on an error by shortstop Mike Bordick.

But Vizcaino was thrown out trying to steal second and later in the inning, Chuck Knoblauch was cut down at the plate. The game belonged to Clemens, whose raw stuff was as good as it was on Oct. 14, when he shut out the Seattle Mariners on one hit and struck out 15. He threw strikes with his first pitch to the first 10 batters he faced.

Clemens went into the clubhouse after that

first inning, and sat alone for more than five minutes. "I knew I had to get control of my emotions quickly," he said later.

The Yankees added another run in the fifth, when Paul O'Neill swung and pulled a looping line drive into the right-field corner, out of Perez's reach, and Martinez scored. Of the six runs scored by the Yankees against the Mets' left-handed starters in the first two games, four of them were driven home by left-handed batters.

The Yankees led, 6–0, in the ninth, and Clemens was removed, having thrown 112 pitches. But the Mets started creeping back, Piazza ripping a two-run homer off Jeff Nelson, and three batters after left fielder Clay Bellinger caught Zeile's fly ball at the fence in left, Jay Payton crushed a three-run homer off Mariano Rivera.

The Yankees' closer finished the game, however, leaving the Mets to figure out how to beat the Yankees, and leaving everyone to wonder what the heck Clemens was thinking about when he caught Piazza's broken bat.

Late life: With Roger Clemens out of the game, the Met bats came to life in the ninth inning, as Mike Piazza (opposite) hit a two-run home run off Jeff Nelson and Jay Payton launched an opposite-field three-run shot off the normally unhittable Mariano Rivera (above).

October 24, 2000 / Mets 4 /Yankees 2

# Home, Sweet Home

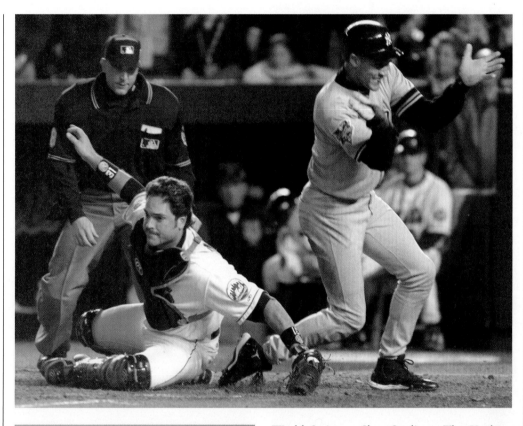

Rick Reed (opposite) gave the Mets six strong innings, allowing only two runs and striking out eight; one of the Yankees' only happy moments was the run scored by Derek Jeter (left) in the third inning after he slid around the tag of catcher Mike Piazza.

| LINE SCORE | | | |
|---|---|---|---|
| Yankees | 0 0 1 | 1 0 0 | 0 0 0 | –2 |
| Mets | 0 1 0 | 0 0 1 | 0 2 x | –4 |

QUEENS—The Subway Series threatened to become an express, a Yankee sweep. But tonight the Mets beat a pitcher who had been unbeatable in the postseason and won a game they had to win.

The Yankees' Orlando Hernandez struck out 12 batters and pitched out of a bases-loaded jam in the sixth inning, but in the eighth, Benny Agbayani snapped a 2–2 tie with a run-scoring double off El Duque, and the Mets prevailed, 4–2, in Game 3 of the World Series at Shea Stadium. The Yankees lead the series, 2–1, but the Mets could even it tomorrow night at Shea.

"It seems like light years' difference between 3–0 and 2–1," said Mets Manager Bobby Valentine, "and it's 2–1."

The defeat broke the Yankees' 14-game World Series winning streak, the longest such streak in championship play among the major sports, and Hernandez's perfect postseason record was blemished. He had been to baseball what Joe Montana was to the Super Bowl, or what Bill Russell was to the National Basketball Association playoffs. When he pitched, the Yankees won, every time. He had made nine

New York native John Franco, replete with an orange sanitation worker's T-shirt under his jersey in tribute to his late father, pitched a scoreless eighth inning before giving way to Armando Benitez in the ninth.

El Duque said he felt O.K. as he dropped a towel over a bag of medication that had just been handed to him.

But the air was warmer than expected at Shea, and Hernandez looked quite comfortable. He and the Mets' Rick Reed, pitchers with superlative control, both took advantage of the large strike zone being called by Jeff Kellogg, the home-plate umpire. Hernandez struck out eight in the first four innings, Reed six in the first two innings.

Robin Ventura crushed a home run off Hernandez in the second, but David Justice drove home Derek Jeter with a two-out double in the third—the relay man Edgardo Alfonzo hesitated on the throw for a moment—and Paul O'Neill tripled to score Tino Martinez in the fourth, giving the Yankees a 2–1 lead.

The Mets still trailed in the sixth, when Mike Piazza led off. Hernandez had thrown sliders to Piazza on the first pitch of his two previous at-bats, and Piazza wound up striking out both times. Hernandez threw another first-pitch slider and Piazza seemed ready, reaching down and smacking a low liner over third base, the ball raising chalk as it struck the baseline before rolling into the corner for a double. Ventura walked. First and second, nobody out.

Todd Zeile pulled a double into the left-field corner, Piazza jogged around third and across home with the tying run while Ventura rambled into third, Zeile into second. The Mets were in business.

Agbayani worked a tough base on balls, ignoring a couple of sliders low and away, and the bases were loaded, the noise level in Shea rising. Jay Payton, Mike Bordick and Reed were due to hit.

Hernandez quickly got ahead in the count against Payton and dispatched him with a slider for a swinging strikeout; one out. He struck out Bordick, whipping a fastball. And he retired the pinch-hitter Darryl Hamilton on a fielder's choice groundout. Hernandez—almost always stoic when he pitches—shouted and raised both fists, pumping them once, twice, three times, short jabs as he walked off the mound, staring toward the ground.

"He took away my aggressiveness and got me out," Payton said. "Then he made some great pitches to Bordick. He's smart, he's got

playoff and World Series starts and pitched in relief once, and the Yankees were 10–0 in those games. Hernandez was 8–0—the most victories without a loss in postseason history, two games better than Lefty Gomez, who went 6–0 for the Yankees from 1932-1939.

There was some question among his teammates about Hernandez's condition for Game 3, for he felt poorly Monday. Asked after the Yankees' workout about whether he was sick,

great stuff, and that's why he's so successful."

Hernandez breezed through the seventh inning, easily retiring the top of the Mets' order. But his spot in the lineup was coming around in the top of the eighth inning, his pitch count was high, about 120, and Yankees Manager Joe Torre was thinking about replacing him.

Hernandez pleaded his case, imploring Torre to leave him in the game, and Torre went along with that, holding up one finger: one more inning. One more inning, for a pitcher in whom he has so much trust, who had never done anything but win in the post-season, high pitch counts or not.

"I was willing to try something else," Torre said afterward, referring to his bullpen, "and he wasn't into that.

"He deserved the right to get a decision in this game. He was pumped, and with what he has done for us, it was tough for me to deny him what he wanted."

Ventura led off the eighth inning and Hernandez struck him out, his 12th of the game, the most ever by a Yankees' pitcher in the World Series, and Torre felt very good about his decision at that point. Zeile, who came into the game with 5 hits in 12 at-bats and had doubled home a run in the sixth, bounced a single through the middle that just bounced over Jeter's glove. Torre still felt comfortable with Hernandez; to the Yankee manager, Zeile hadn't really hit the ball that hard.

Agbayani was next. All he had heard about the last two days, he said afterward, was how the Yankees hadn't lost a World Series game in four years, and how Hernandez

**Todd Zeile, the Mets' most effective hitter in the postseason, doubled in Mike Piazza with the game-tying run in the sixth inning.**

had been so extraordinary in the postseason.

With one swing, Agbayani changed all that. Hernandez threw a fastball over the middle and Agbayani tagged it, driving the ball all the way to the wall in left-center, Zeile scoring, the stands at Shea Stadium shaking with emotion. Agbayani looked once at the sky, one very long look. Hernandez stared around the field. He had an unfamiliar feeling in the postseason: he was losing.

Joe McEwing pinch-ran for Agbayani and, after Payton's infield hit knocked out Hernandez, Bubba Trammell pinch-hit against Mike Stanton and lifted a sacrifice fly, increasing the Mets' lead to 4–2.

John Franco had pitched the eighth inning for the Mets, but he stayed in the dugout to watch the ninth, jacket pulled up high. Armando Benitez, who had blown a one-run lead in the ninth inning of Game 1, jogged in from the bullpen. Trouble began immediately for the Mets: Chuck Kno-

Fan darling Benny Agbayani (opposite, below) ripped a line drive into left-center field to score Todd Zeile (opposite, above) with the go-ahead run in the eighth inning before Armando Benitez (left) entered the game and closed the door in the ninth.

blauch, pinch-hitting, rifled a single to center.

But Benitez retired Jose Vizcaino on a fly to center, and struck out Jeter on a fastball across the outside corner. Benitez fell behind Justice, 3–1, but battled back, and when Justice popped the ball to the right side, Benitez pointed a finger into the air happily, pointing at the pop for all to see.

The Mets had gone where no team had gone before and conquered El Duque in the postseason. They will know, in the next five days, if they can do the same to the Yankees.

# Taking Charge

Opening statement: Bobby J. Jones (left) could only watch helplessly as a first-pitch blast off the bat of Derek Jeter (opposite) disappeared into the outer reaches of Shea Stadium.

**LINE SCORE**

| | | | | | | | | | | | |
|---|---|---|---|---|---|---|---|---|---|---|---|
| Yankees | 1 1 1 | 0 0 0 | 0 0 0 | –3 |
| Mets | 0 0 2 | 0 0 0 | 0 0 0 | –2 |

**QUEENS**—The Mets needed to build on the momentum of their Game 3 victory, but it didn't even last a single pitch in Game 4 of the Subway Series tonight. Derek Jeter clubbed Bobby J. Jones's first offering of the game for a home run, giving the Yankees a lead they never relinquished, and now the Yankees are on the verge of another championship.

A relay team of Yankees' relievers—David Cone, Jeff Nelson, Mike Stanton and Mariano Rivera—maintained a 3–2 lead from the fifth inning through the ninth at Shea Stadium, giving the Yankees a 3–1 lead in the series. Jeter added a triple to his home run and scored twice, and Paul O'Neill, 37, who has been revitalized in this Series, had a triple and single and made a sliding catch to start the bottom of the eighth inning.

Cone got one out in the fifth in relief of Denny Neagle. Nelson got four outs, Stanton two, and Rivera came on to pitch the final two innings for the Yankees. "They made a lot of good pitches, especially out of the bullpen," said Bobby Valentine, the Mets' manager.

The Yankees staggered and nearly collapsed at the end of the regular season and

**Though he had allowed only two runs, Denny Neagle (above) was not allowed to pitch to Mike Piazza in the fifth inning; Joe Torre removed him in favor of David Cone, who made his only appearance in the series.**

barely got through the first round of the playoffs against the Oakland Athletics. They play with the knowledge that some of the veterans who have been integral to the recent championships probably won't be in pinstripes next year. But now they are one victory away from becoming the first team since the Athletics of 1972–74 to win three consecutive championships, and the first team to do so since the advent of free agency in 1976, a change that made it far more difficult for clubs to hold a core of players together.

Yankees Manager Joe Torre juggled his lineup a little for Game 4, replacing Jose Vizcaino with Luis Sojo at second base and reluctantly shifting Derek Jeter to the leadoff spot. Jeter is the antithesis of the prototypical leadoff hitter, an aggressive swinger more likely to hack at the first pitch than wait patiently, and Torre strongly prefers using him as his No. 2 hitter. But with Chuck Knoblauch out of the lineup, Jeter was Torre's best option.

Jones, the Mets' starter, usually has good control and pitches around the strike zone, but he started the game with a twist, throwing a changeup with his first pitch rather than a fastball.

Just before Jones threw the pitch, Knoblauch

made a prediction on the Yankees' bench: "First pitch is going out." Vizcaino and a couple of others on the Yankee bench heard it.

Jeter attacked the first pitch and launched a high drive to left field, and before everybody was seated at Shea Stadium, the Yankees led by 1–0. It was, Torre said later, a huge lift, a relief.

Some of the Yankees fell out of the dugout laughing. Vizcaino pointed at Knoblauch, and as soon as Jeter returned to the dugout, breathing heavily from excitement, Knoblauch sat next to him and filled him in.

"It was just a feeling," Knoblauch said afterward. "You say it and you see what happens. You look smart when it happens."

And if you were among the Yankees, you were off and running. "We wanted to take the

crowd out of it," Jeter said. "We wanted to get some runs early."

The Yankees quickly added two more, O'Neill tripling and scoring on a sacrifice fly in the second, Jeter slamming a triple and coming home on a ground ball when the Mets elected to play the infield back with nobody out.

Neagle was armed with a three-run lead in a situation similar to the one he faced in Game 4 of the 1996 World Series. Pitching for the Atlanta Braves in that game, Neagle had a 6–0 lead and was knocked out in the sixth. Two innings later, Jim Leyritz hammered a three-run homer off Mark Wohlers to tie the game, and the Yankees went on to win the championship.

Neagle shut out the Mets in the first two innings tonight, but not flawlessly—he walked

a couple of batters, and in the first inning, he threw a 78-mile-an-hour changeup over the middle of the plate that Mike Piazza launched about 420 feet, foul.

Timo Perez singled through the middle to start the third for the Mets, Neagle dropping to the ground to avoid the line drive, and took second as Edgardo Alfonzo grounded to third. Then Piazza extended his arms and slammed a two-run homer, cutting the Yankees' lead to 3–2.

Piazza's monstrous foul ball and his home run off Neagle apparently weighed heavily on Torre, and as the Mets prepared to hit in the top of the fifth, a call went down to the Yankees' bullpen. Cone was told to warm up, to prepare to pitch to Piazza. Neagle retired the first two batters with easy fly balls.

**O'Neill revival: A resurgent Paul O'Neill chugged around the bases for a triple in the second inning that led to the Yankees' second run.**

**Mike Piazza's two-run blast in the third inning (above) brought the Mets within a run and convinced Joe Torre that he did not want Denny Neagle to face him again.**

One out away from qualifying for a victory, Neagle stood behind the mound rubbing up a baseball, preparing to pitch to Piazza, and that was when he saw Torre stepping out of the Yankees' dugout and pointing his right hand toward the Yankees' bullpen, summoning Cone. Neagle was stunned, and he turned and glanced toward the scoreboard: yes, the Yankees led, 3–2, and yes, he was one out away from finishing his fifth inning. He was finished for the night, and he was furious, handing the ball to Torre without looking at him.

Cone, 37, jogged and then walked in from the visitors' bullpen for his first appearance in Shea Stadium since the Mets traded him to the Toronto Blue Jays in August 1992, curious at the response he would receive. "It was pretty firm boos," Cone said. "I know where I stand now."

Pitching from the stretch, Cone threw Piazza sharp sliders, and Piazza popped out to second. It was the beginning and the end for Cone, who was removed for a pinch-hitter in the top of the sixth, but the Yankees couldn't score in that inning, or any other. By the end of the night they would extend their streak of hitless at-bats with runners in scoring position to 14, and they would strand nine more runners, giving them 46 for the first four games.

But Nelson relieved in the sixth, shutting out the Mets in that inning and striking out the leadoff batter in the seventh. After he walked a pinch-hitter, Lenny Harris, the left-hander Mike Stanton came on and pitched to Bubba Trammell, another pinch-hitter, and struck him out on a high fastball. Kurt Abbott was inserted as a

**Derek Jeter (left) tripled, then scored the Yankees' third and final run in the third inning; with Mariano Rivera (below) waiting in the bullpen it was all the Yankees would need, as the Mets managed only one base runner off him in the final two innings.**

pinch-hitter for Perez—Valentine was doing all he could to score in that inning, knowing that the nearly unhittable Rivera loomed in the bullpen—and Stanton struck him out, as well.

Rivera came on to pitch the eighth, holding the Mets scoreless as O'Neill made a sliding catch on Alfonzo to open the inning. To start the ninth, Rivera buzzed a fastball over the inside corner to Benny Agbayani for a strike-out, rather than throwing his cutter outside, as right-handed hitters now expect him to do. He then retired Jay Payton on a fly ball.

Matt Franco walked to the plate to pinch-hit. In July 1999, Franco had beaten Rivera with a two-run, two-out single in the bottom of the ninth at Shea, sending the stadium into a frenzy. But Rivera was in control here, throwing his hardest fastball of his two innings for the first strike before zipping a fastball to finish off Franco on a called third strike.

Sometime in the middle of the game, a pipe broke in the Yankees' clubhouse and flooded it, and as Torre headed back to the clubhouse, he had no idea of what he would find, whether there would be inches of standing water.

"But right now," he said, smiling, "I don't care."

# The Dynasty

**Going deep: The Yankees used a pair of solo home runs, the first from Bernie Williams in the second inning (opposite), and the second by Derek Jeter in the sixth (right) to produce their first two runs.**

| LINE SCORE | | | | | | | | | |
|---|---|---|---|---|---|---|---|---|---|
| **Yankees** | 0 | 1 | 0 | 0 | 0 | 1 | 0 | 0 | 2 | –4 |
| **Mets** | 0 | 2 | 0 | 0 | 0 | 0 | 0 | 0 | 0 | –2 |

QUEENS—The Yankees maintained their preeminence in New York last night, finishing off the Mets in the Subway Series by rallying in the ninth inning of Game 5, and established their place among the greatest baseball dynasties by winning their third consecutive title.

Luis Sojo slapped a rolling single off the Mets' starting pitcher, Al Leiter, with two outs in the top of the ninth to score Jorge Posada with the tie-breaking run, and when the throw home bounced off Posada and rolled into the Mets' dugout, Scott Brosius also scored. The Yankees won, 4–2, at Shea Stadium, finishing off a breathless World Series in which three games were decided by one run, two others by two runs.

When Mike Piazza flied out to deep center field to end the game—coming within 15 feet or so of hitting a game-tying home run—center fielder Bernie Williams dropped to a knee in prayer, then jumped and hugged left fielder Clay Bellinger, as teammates rushed from the Yankees' dugout to swarm the infield, to join the closer, Mariano Rivera, and Derek Jeter, the World Series most valuable player, and the rest.

Some players lifted Manager Joe Torre onto their shoulders and carried him off the field; the principal owner, George Steinbrenner, watching the final out in the clubhouse, burst into tears. "The Mets gave us everything we could want," he said, "and it was great for New York."

After winning the World Series 25 times in the 1900's, the Yankees have won again.

The Mets advanced further into the post-season than they had in more than a decade,

The Mets manufactured a pair of runs in the second inning, the key play being a drag bunt by Al Leiter that the Yankees misplayed, allowing Leiter to reach safely and Bubba Trammell to score the Mets' first run.

and there will be some solace in that. But for their fans, this is the worst imaginable fate: not only did the Mets lose the World Series, but they were also beaten by their cross-city rivals; this was the big brother whipping the little brother in a snowball fight and then rubbing his face in the slush, an indelible memory that can be mitigated only by revenge that may not come for years, or may never come.

"There are a lot of heavy hearts in that clubhouse," Mets Manager Bobby Valentine said, "and I have a heavy heart with them."

The Mets were in position to win this game, as they were in all the games. After Williams homered in the top of the second, breaking a streak of 22 consecutive hitless at-bats, the Yankees misplayed a surprise bunt by Leiter in the second inning and the Mets scored twice, taking a 2–1 lead.

Trying to lead the Mets back into the Series, Leiter pitched aggressively, brushing

back both Paul O'Neill and David Justice early. He drove back Jeter with a fastball in the sixth inning, and Jeter—who led off Game 3 with a homer and later tripled—bashed a game-tying homer, sending the ball into the back of the visitors' bullpen in left field.

Andy Pettitte pitched the first seven innings for the Yankees and was relieved by Mike Stanton in the eighth, the score still tied at 2–2. Leiter threw 121 pitches in the first eight innings, but just as Yankees Manager Joe Torre stuck with Orlando Hernandez in the Yankees' Game 3 loss, Valentine stayed with his ace, and Leiter struck out Tino Martinez and O'Neill to start the ninth inning. "I thought he was looking good at that point," Valentine said.

But Posada fouled off three pitches with two strikes and coaxed a walk from Leiter, on his 138th pitch. Brosius lined a single to left on Leiter's 141st pitch—six more pitches than Leiter had thrown in any other game

this season—and Posada stopped at second.

John Franco was warming up in the bullpen for the Mets, ready to come in; Valentine was somewhat concerned about calling on Franco for a third straight day, for Franco pitched in Games 3 and 4.

Sojo, who had entered the game in the eighth inning, was due to bat. But then Glenallen Hill stepped out of the Yankees' dugout, with 6 hits in 13 career at-bats against Franco, including three homers, and stood in the on-deck circle.

Valentine considered his options: the tiring Leiter against Sojo, or Franco, knowing that Hill could be used to pinch-hit for Sojo.

Valentine stuck with Leiter, who threw a fastball to Sojo—one of a horde of players acquired during the season by the Yankees' front office—and Sojo bounced Leiter's 142nd pitch through the middle, a bounding ball.

"I said to El Duque, 'I want to hit with a man on base,' " Sojo said. He said the first-base coach, Lee Mazzilli, told him, "Stay back, trust

**The second-inning bunt by Al Leiter was mishandled at the beginning and end of the play as Tino Martinez bobbled the ball before fielding it and Andy Pettitte (above) couldn't handle the throw when it finally arrived.**

your hands, try to hit the ball up the middle."

Sojo said, "All my career, I don't hit Al Leiter good."

The Yankees' players rushed forward from the dugout, to the front steps, the whole play in front of them. Posada rounded third and looked over his left shoulder to see whether he might be able to beat the throw from center fielder Jay Payton. The ball and the runner would arrive at the same time.

Waiting at the plate for the throw, Piazza had to make a choice in a millisecond. He could either hold his ground and try to block home, or he could step out in front of the plate and reach for the throw and give Posada an opening to slide across the plate.

Piazza planted himself on the baseline, Posada veered toward the mound and the throw hit him and skipped into the Mets' dugout. Brosius was waved home by the umpires, though Valentine would argue about whether Brosius should have been awarded the extra base.

The gutsy Al Leiter ran out of steam in the ninth inning, allowing a walk to Jorge Posada, a single by Scott Brosius and the game-winning hit from Luis Sojo (above), which left Leiter a saddened spectator on the mound (right); with the game and the Yankees' 26th World Series title firmly in hand, Mariano Rivera (opposite) was jubilation incarnate as he leapt skyward in celebration.

Now Rivera jogged in from the bullpen to pitch the ninth inning. Players on other teams believe he has been the difference between the Yankees' being a great team, like the Atlanta Braves, and a team that wins the championship every year. Rivera, his fastball juiced a couple of miles an hour faster than in Game 4 by the adrenaline, struck out the pinch-hitter Darryl Hamilton.

He walked Benny Agbayani, but Edgardo Alfonzo flied to right. Agbayani, uncontested by the Yankees, had advanced to third by this point, and Piazza went to the plate as the potential tying run. Jeter went to the mound, slapped Rivera with his glove, probably telling him he was the best and to finish it off, something Jeter tells him all the time.

Rivera fired a fastball, and Piazza—who had just missed several high fastballs during this Series—blistered a high drive toward center field, a baseball riding a home run parabola. "Nooo!" Torre shouted in the dugout.

But Williams said: "I knew right away. I knew he didn't hit it."

Williams ran back toward the wall, then turned, set himself and made the catch, and at midnight, the first Subway Series in 44 years was over. The Yankees went crazy. Rivera turned and raised his arms and jumped, until Martinez reached him, and Posada; O'Neill ran in from right field, glancing at the sky, on the first anniversary of his father's death; Jeter and Sojo were hugging near second base, and Torre was in the dugout, hugging his coaches. After Torre was hoisted on his players' shoulders, he walked to the stands and summoned his wife, and they embraced and kissed, Torre's eyes watering.

"I'd be lying if I said this one wasn't more gratifying," Jeter said afterward. "I mean, we struggled this year. We had tough times."

Posada said, "They don't get old, I'm telling you that."

A half hour after the game, many of the Yankees began to stream out of the clubhouse and onto the field, their shirts soaked with Champagne, and they held the championship trophy aloft, Roger Clemens and O'Neill and others. Fans who remained at Shea Stadium chanted O'Neill's named and thanked him, thanked all of them. Four titles in five years, a city's dynasty.

# True Believers

In the white heat of the Subway Series, fans of every stripe got into the act, making their allegiances abundantly clear through signs, face painting, and, in some cases, through a tribute to a favorite player. (Is that Mike Piazza in the knit cap above?)

In the wake of the Clemens-Piazza bat incident, emotions ran high, as illustrated by the Met fan at left; for many Yankee fans, the incident was a mere distraction to their primary goal: a World Series threepeat.

THE LUCKIEST FANS ON THE FACE OF THE EARTH

As has always been the case, autographs were fervently sought throughout the series, particularly by the younger set; in the end, fans on both sides of the great metropolitan divide came to realize their good fortune in witnessing a Subway Series.

# Appendix

**NEW YORK YANKEES**

| BATTING | BA | G | AB | R | H | TB | 2B | 3B | HR | RBI | SB | BB | SO |
|---|---|---|---|---|---|---|---|---|---|---|---|---|---|
| Jeter, Derek | .339 | 148 | 593 | 119 | 201 | 285 | 31 | 4 | 15 | 73 | 22 | 68 | 99 |
| Williams, Bernie | .307 | 141 | 537 | 108 | 165 | 304 | 37 | 6 | 30 | 121 | 13 | 71 | 84 |
| Hill, Glenallen | .293 | 104 | 300 | 45 | 88 | 180 | 9 | 1 | 27 | 58 | 0 | 19 | 76 |
| Posada, Jorge | .287 | 151 | 505 | 92 | 145 | 266 | 35 | 1 | 28 | 86 | 2 | 107 | 151 |
| Justice, David | .286 | 146 | 524 | 89 | 150 | 306 | 31 | 1 | 41 | 118 | 2 | 77 | 91 |
| Sojo, Luis | .286 | 95 | 301 | 33 | 86 | 127 | 18 | 1 | 7 | 37 | 2 | 17 | 22 |
| O'Neill, Paul | .283 | 142 | 566 | 79 | 160 | 240 | 26 | 0 | 18 | 100 | 14 | 51 | 90 |
| Knoblauch, Chuck | .283 | 102 | 400 | 75 | 113 | 154 | 22 | 2 | 5 | 26 | 15 | 46 | 45 |
| Spencer, Shane | .282 | 73 | 248 | 33 | 70 | 114 | 11 | 3 | 9 | 40 | 1 | 19 | 45 |
| Polonia, Luis | .276 | 117 | 344 | 48 | 95 | 140 | 14 | 5 | 7 | 30 | 12 | 29 | 32 |
| Martinez, Tino | .258 | 155 | 569 | 69 | 147 | 240 | 37 | 4 | 16 | 91 | 4 | 52 | 74 |
| Canseco, Jose | .252 | 98 | 329 | 47 | 83 | 146 | 18 | 0 | 15 | 49 | 2 | 64 | 102 |
| Vizcaino, Jose | .251 | 113 | 267 | 32 | 67 | 81 | 10 | 2 | 0 | 14 | 6 | 22 | 43 |
| Brosius, Scott | .230 | 135 | 470 | 57 | 108 | 176 | 20 | 0 | 16 | 64 | 0 | 45 | 73 |
| Bellinger, Clay | .207 | 98 | 184 | 33 | 38 | 68 | 8 | 2 | 6 | 21 | 5 | 17 | 48 |
| TOTALS | .277 | 161 | 5556 | 871 | 1541 | 2500 | 294 | 25 | 205 | 833 | 99 | 631 | 1007 |

| PITCHING | ERA | W | L | G | GS | CG | SV | INN | H | R | ER | BB | SO |
|---|---|---|---|---|---|---|---|---|---|---|---|---|---|
| Nelson, Jeff | 2.45 | 8 | 4 | 73 | 0 | 0 | 0 | 69⅓ | 44 | 24 | 19 | 45 | 71 |
| Rivera, Mariano | 2.85 | 7 | 4 | 66 | 0 | 0 | 36 | 75⅓ | 58 | 26 | 24 | 25 | 58 |
| Clemens, Roger | 3.70 | 13 | 8 | 32 | 32 | 1 | 0 | 204⅓ | 184 | 96 | 84 | 84 | 188 |
| Stanton, Mike | 4.10 | 2 | 3 | 69 | 0 | 0 | 0 | 68 | 68 | 32 | 31 | 24 | 75 |
| Mendoza, Ramiro | 4.25 | 7 | 4 | 14 | 9 | 1 | 0 | 65⅔ | 66 | 32 | 31 | 20 | 30 |
| Pettitte, Andy | 4.35 | 19 | 9 | 32 | 32 | 3 | 0 | 204⅔ | 219 | 111 | 99 | 80 | 125 |
| Hernandez, Orlando | 4.51 | 12 | 13 | 29 | 29 | 3 | 0 | 195⅔ | 186 | 104 | 98 | 51 | 141 |
| Neagle, Denny | 4.52 | 15 | 9 | 34 | 33 | 1 | 0 | 209 | 210 | 109 | 105 | 81 | 146 |
| Gooden, Dwight | 4.71 | 6 | 5 | 27 | 14 | 0 | 2 | 105 | 119 | 64 | 55 | 44 | 55 |
| Grimsley, Jason | 5.04 | 3 | 2 | 63 | 4 | 0 | 1 | 96⅓ | 100 | 58 | 54 | 42 | 53 |
| Cone, David | 6.91 | 4 | 14 | 30 | 29 | 0 | 0 | 155 | 192 | 124 | 119 | 82 | 120 |
| TOTALS | 4.76 | 87 | 74 | 161 | 161 | 9 | 40 | 1424⅓ | 1458 | 814 | 753 | 577 | 1040 |

**NEW YORK METS**

| BATTING | BA | G | AB | R | H | TB | 2B | 3B | HR | RBI | SB | BB | SO |
|---|---|---|---|---|---|---|---|---|---|---|---|---|---|
| Alfonzo, Edgardo | .324 | 150 | 544 | 109 | 176 | 295 | 40 | 2 | 25 | 94 | 3 | 95 | 70 |
| Piazza, Mike | .324 | 136 | 482 | 90 | 156 | 296 | 26 | 0 | 38 | 113 | 4 | 58 | 69 |
| Payton, Jay | .291 | 149 | 488 | 63 | 142 | 218 | 23 | 1 | 17 | 62 | 5 | 30 | 60 |
| Agbayani, Benny | .289 | 119 | 350 | 59 | 101 | 168 | 19 | 1 | 15 | 60 | 5 | 54 | 68 |
| Bordick, Mike | .285 | 156 | 583 | 88 | 166 | 258 | 30 | 1 | 20 | 80 | 9 | 49 | 99 |
| Pratt, Todd | .275 | 80 | 160 | 33 | 44 | 74 | 6 | 0 | 8 | 25 | 0 | 22 | 31 |
| Zeile, Todd | .268 | 153 | 544 | 67 | 146 | 254 | 36 | 3 | 22 | 79 | 3 | 74 | 85 |
| Bell, Derek | .266 | 144 | 546 | 87 | 145 | 232 | 31 | 1 | 18 | 69 | 8 | 65 | 125 |
| Trammell, Bubba | .265 | 102 | 245 | 28 | 65 | 112 | 13 | 2 | 10 | 45 | 4 | 29 | 49 |
| Harris, Lenny | .260 | 112 | 223 | 31 | 58 | 85 | 7 | 4 | 4 | 26 | 13 | 20 | 22 |
| Franco, Matt | .239 | 101 | 134 | 9 | 32 | 42 | 4 | 0 | 2 | 14 | 0 | 21 | 22 |
| Ventura, Robin | .232 | 141 | 469 | 61 | 109 | 206 | 23 | 1 | 24 | 84 | 3 | 75 | 91 |
| McEwing, Joe | .222 | 87 | 153 | 20 | 34 | 56 | 14 | 1 | 2 | 19 | 3 | 5 | 29 |
| Abbott, Kurt | .217 | 79 | 157 | 22 | 34 | 61 | 7 | 1 | 6 | 12 | 1 | 14 | 51 |
| TOTALS | .263 | 162 | 5486 | 807 | 1445 | 2360 | 281 | 20 | 198 | 761 | 66 | 675 | 1037 |

| PITCHING | ERA | W | L | G | GS | CG | SV | INN | H | R | ER | BB | SO |
|---|---|---|---|---|---|---|---|---|---|---|---|---|---|
| Benitez, Armando | 2.61 | 4 | 4 | 76 | 0 | 0 | 41 | 76 | 39 | 24 | 22 | 38 | 106 |
| Hampton, Mike | 3.14 | 15 | 10 | 33 | 33 | 3 | 0 | 217⅔ | 194 | 89 | 76 | 99 | 151 |
| Leiter, Al | 3.20 | 16 | 8 | 31 | 31 | 2 | 0 | 208 | 176 | 84 | 74 | 76 | 200 |
| Franco, John | 3.40 | 5 | 4 | 62 | 0 | 0 | 4 | 55⅔ | 46 | 24 | 21 | 26 | 56 |
| White, Rick | 3.52 | 5 | 9 | 66 | 0 | 0 | 3 | 99⅔ | 83 | 44 | 39 | 38 | 67 |
| Wendell, Turk | 3.59 | 8 | 6 | 77 | 0 | 0 | 1 | 82⅔ | 60 | 36 | 33 | 41 | 73 |
| Rusch, Glendon | 4.01 | 11 | 11 | 31 | 30 | 2 | 0 | 190⅔ | 196 | 91 | 85 | 44 | 157 |
| Reed, Rick | 4.11 | 11 | 5 | 30 | 30 | 0 | 0 | 184 | 192 | 90 | 84 | 34 | 121 |
| Jones, Bobby J. | 5.06 | 11 | 6 | 27 | 27 | 1 | 0 | 154⅔ | 171 | 90 | 87 | 49 | 85 |
| Cook, Dennis | 5.34 | 6 | 3 | 68 | 0 | 0 | 2 | 59 | 63 | 35 | 35 | 31 | 53 |
| Mahomes, Pat | 5.46 | 5 | 3 | 53 | 5 | 0 | 0 | 94 | 96 | 63 | 57 | 66 | 76 |
| TOTALS | 4.16 | 94 | 68 | 162 | 162 | 8 | 49 | 1450 | 1398 | 738 | 670 | 574 | 1164 |

## AMERICAN LEAGUE DIVISION SERIES COMPOSITE BOX SCORE

### NEW YORK YANKEES

| BATTING | AB | R | H | HR | RBI | Avg |
|---|---|---|---|---|---|---|
| Bellinger | 1 | 0 | 1 | 0 | 1 | 1.000 |
| Polonia | 1 | 0 | 1 | 0 | 0 | 1.000 |
| Martinez | 19 | 2 | 8 | 0 | 4 | .421 |
| Knoblauch | 9 | 1 | 3 | 0 | 1 | .333 |
| Williams | 20 | 3 | 5 | 0 | 1 | .250 |
| Posada | 17 | 2 | 4 | 0 | 1 | .235 |
| Justice | 18 | 2 | 4 | 1 | 1 | .222 |
| Jeter | 19 | 1 | 4 | 0 | 2 | .211 |
| O'Neill | 19 | 4 | 4 | 0 | 0 | .211 |
| Sojo | 16 | 2 | 3 | 0 | 5 | .188 |
| Brosius | 17 | 0 | 3 | 0 | 1 | .176 |
| Hill | 12 | 1 | 1 | 0 | 2 | .083 |
| Vizcaino | 0 | 1 | 0 | 0 | 0 | .000 |
| TOTALS | 168 | 19 | 41 | 1 | 19 | .244 |

| PITCHING | G | IP | H | BB | SO | ERA |
|---|---|---|---|---|---|---|
| Rivera | 3 | 5 | 2 | 0 | 2 | 0.00 |
| Nelson | 2 | 2 | 0 | 0 | 2 | 0.00 |
| Stanton | 3 | 4⅓ | 5 | 1 | 3 | 2.08 |
| O. Hernandez | 2 | 7⅓ | 5 | 5 | 5 | 2.45 |
| Pettitte | 2 | 11⅓ | 15 | 3 | 7 | 3.97 |
| Choate | 1 | 1⅓ | 0 | 1 | 1 | 6.75 |
| Clemens | 2 | 11 | 13 | 8 | 10 | 8.18 |
| TOTALS | 5 | 44 | 44 | 19 | 31 | 4.70 |

### OAKLAND ATHLETICS

| BATTING | AB | R | H | HR | RBI | Avg |
|---|---|---|---|---|---|---|
| Porter | 1 | 0 | 1 | 0 | 1 | 1.000 |
| Christenson | 2 | 0 | 1 | 0 | 1 | .500 |
| R. Hernandez | 16 | 3 | 6 | 0 | 3 | .375 |
| Tejada | 20 | 5 | 7 | 0 | 1 | .350 |
| Chavez | 21 | 4 | 7 | 0 | 4 | .333 |
| Je. Giambi | 9 | 1 | 3 | 0 | 1 | .333 |
| Ja. Giambi | 14 | 2 | 4 | 0 | 1 | .286 |
| Velarde | 20 | 2 | 5 | 0 | 3 | .250 |
| Saenz | 13 | 1 | 3 | 1 | 4 | .231 |
| Piatt | 6 | 2 | 1 | 0 | 0 | .167 |
| Long | 19 | 2 | 3 | 1 | 1 | .158 |
| Grieve | 17 | 1 | 2 | 0 | 2 | .118 |
| TOTALS | 167 | 23 | 44 | 2 | 22 | .263 |

| PITCHING | G | IP | H | BB | SO | ERA |
|---|---|---|---|---|---|---|
| Mecir | 3 | 5⅓ | 1 | 0 | 2 | 0.00 |
| Magante | 2 | 3 | 1 | 0 | 2 | 0.00 |
| Tam | 3 | 2 | 3 | 1 | 1 | 0.00 |
| Isringhausen | 2 | 2 | 1 | 0 | 3 | 0.00 |
| Jones | 2 | 1⅓ | 1 | 0 | 1 | 0.00 |
| Zito | 1 | 5⅔ | 7 | 2 | 5 | 1.59 |
| Hudson | 1 | 8 | 6 | 4 | 5 | 3.38 |
| Appier | 2 | 10⅓ | 10 | 6 | 13 | 3.48 |
| TOTALS | 5 | 44 | 41 | 16 | 35 | 3.48 |

## NATIONAL LEAGUE DIVISION SERIES COMPOSITE BOX SCORE

### NEW YORK METS

| BATTING | AB | R | H | HR | RBI | Avg |
|---|---|---|---|---|---|---|
| McEwing | 1 | 0 | 1 | 0 | 0 | 1.000 |
| Hamilton | 4 | 1 | 2 | 0 | 0 | .500 |
| Hampton | 2 | 0 | 1 | 0 | 0 | .500 |
| Agbayani | 15 | 1 | 5 | 1 | 1 | .333 |
| Perez | 17 | 2 | 5 | 0 | 3 | .294 |
| Alfonzo | 18 | 1 | 5 | 1 | 5 | .278 |
| Piazza | 14 | 1 | 3 | 0 | 0 | .214 |
| Payton | 17 | 1 | 3 | 0 | 2 | .176 |
| Bordick | 12 | 3 | 2 | 0 | 0 | .167 |
| Ventura | 14 | 1 | 2 | 1 | 2 | .143 |
| Zeile | 14 | 0 | 1 | 0 | 0 | .071 |
| B.J. Jones | 4 | 1 | 0 | 0 | 0 | .000 |
| Harris | 2 | 1 | 0 | 0 | 0 | .000 |
| Abbott | 2 | 0 | 0 | 0 | 0 | .000 |
| TOTALS | 143 | 13 | 30 | 3 | 13 | .210 |

| PITCHING | G | IP | H | BB | SO | ERA |
|---|---|---|---|---|---|---|
| B.J. Jones | 1 | 9 | 1 | 2 | 5 | 0.00 |
| White | 2 | 2⅔ | 6 | 0 | 4 | 0.00 |
| Leiter | 1 | 8 | 5 | 3 | 6 | 2.25 |
| Reed | 1 | 6 | 7 | 2 | 6 | 3.00 |
| Hampton | 1 | 5⅓ | 6 | 3 | 2 | 8.44 |
| Benitez | 2 | 3 | 4 | 1 | 3 | 6.00 |
| TOTALS | 4 | 40 | 30 | 16 | 36 | 2.48 |

### SAN FRANCISCO GIANTS

| BATTING | AB | R | H | HR | RBI | Avg |
|---|---|---|---|---|---|---|
| Rios | 2 | 0 | 1 | 0 | 0 | .500 |
| Snow | 10 | 1 | 4 | 1 | 3 | .400 |
| Kent | 16 | 3 | 6 | 0 | 1 | .375 |
| Martinez | 6 | 0 | 2 | 0 | 0 | .333 |
| Mueller | 20 | 2 | 5 | 0 | 0 | .250 |
| Crespo | 4 | 0 | 1 | 0 | 0 | .250 |
| Burks | 13 | 2 | 3 | 1 | 4 | .231 |
| Murray | 5 | 0 | 1 | 0 | 0 | .200 |
| Bonds | 17 | 2 | 3 | 0 | 1 | .176 |
| Aurilia | 15 | 0 | 2 | 0 | 0 | .133 |
| Estalella | 12 | 1 | 1 | 0 | 1 | .083 |
| Benard | 14 | 0 | 1 | 0 | 1 | .071 |
| TOTALS | 146 | 11 | 30 | 2 | 11 | .205 |

| PITCHING | G | IP | H | BB | SO | ERA |
|---|---|---|---|---|---|---|
| Rueter | 1 | 4⅓ | 3 | 1 | 1 | 0.00 |
| Nen | 2 | 2⅓ | 2 | 1 | 3 | 0.00 |
| L. Hernandez | 1 | 7⅔ | 5 | 5 | 5 | 1.17 |
| Ortiz | 1 | 5⅓ | 2 | 4 | 4 | 1.69 |
| Henry | 3 | 4 | 1 | 3 | 1 | 2.25 |
| Estes | 1 | 3 | 3 | 3 | 3 | 6.00 |
| Rodriguez | 2 | 4⅓ | 6 | 1 | 6 | 6.23 |
| Gardner | 1 | 4⅓ | 4 | 2 | 5 | 8.31 |
| TOTALS | 4 | 41 | 30 | 20 | 30 | 2.97 |

## AMERICAN LEAGUE CHAMPIONSHIP SERIES COMPOSITE BOX SCORE

### NEW YORK YANKEES

| BATTING | AB | R | H | HR | RBI | Avg |
|---|---|---|---|---|---|---|
| Vizcaino | 2 | 3 | 2 | 0 | 2 | 1.000 |
| Williams | 23 | 5 | 10 | 1 | 3 | .435 |
| Martinez | 23 | 5 | 8 | 1 | 1 | .320 |
| Jeter | 22 | 6 | 7 | 2 | 5 | .318 |
| Knoblauch | 23 | 3 | 6 | 0 | 2 | .261 |
| Sojo | 23 | 1 | 6 | 0 | 2 | .261 |
| O'Neill | 20 | 0 | 5 | 0 | 5 | .250 |
| Justice | 26 | 4 | 6 | 2 | 8 | .231 |
| Brosius | 18 | 2 | 4 | 0 | 0 | .222 |
| Posada | 19 | 2 | 3 | 0 | 3 | .158 |
| Hill | 2 | 0 | 0 | 0 | 0 | .000 |
| Polonia | 1 | 0 | 0 | 0 | 0 | .000 |
| Bellinger | 0 | 0 | 0 | 0 | 0 | — |
| TOTALS | 204 | 31 | 57 | 6 | 31 | .279 |

| PITCHING | G | IP | H | BB | SO | ERA |
|---|---|---|---|---|---|---|
| Clemens | 1 | 9 | 1 | 2 | 15 | 0.00 |
| Gooden | 1 | 2⅓ | 1 | 0 | 1 | 0.00 |
| Grimsley | 2 | 1 | 2 | 3 | 1 | 0.00 |
| Cone | 1 | 1 | 0 | 0 | 0 | 0.00 |
| Choate | 1 | ⅓ | 0 | 0 | 1 | 0.00 |
| Rivera | 3 | 4⅔ | 4 | 0 | 4 | 1.93 |
| Pettitte | 1 | 6⅔ | 9 | 1 | 2 | 2.70 |
| Hernandez | 2 | 15 | 13 | 8 | 14 | 4.20 |
| Neagle | 3 | 3 | 5 | 0 | 6 | 4.50 |
| Nelson | 3 | 3 | 5 | 0 | 6 | 9.00 |
| TOTALS | 6 | 53 | 41 | 21 | 48 | 3.06 |

### SEATTLE MARINERS

| BATTING | AB | R | H | HR | RBI | Avg |
|---|---|---|---|---|---|---|
| Rodriguez | 22 | 4 | 9 | 2 | 5 | .409 |
| Olerud | 20 | 3 | 7 | 1 | 2 | .350 |
| McLemore | 16 | 2 | 4 | 0 | 2 | .250 |
| Martinez | 21 | 2 | 5 | 1 | 4 | .238 |
| Bell | 18 | 0 | 4 | 0 | 0 | .222 |
| Henderson | 9 | 2 | 2 | 0 | 1 | .222 |
| Guillen | 5 | 1 | 1 | 1 | 2 | .200 |
| Buhner | 11 | 0 | 2 | 0 | 0 | .182 |
| Martin | 11 | 1 | 2 | 0 | 0 | .182 |
| Oliver | 6 | 0 | 1 | 0 | 0 | .167 |
| Cameron | 18 | 3 | 2 | 0 | 1 | .111 |
| Wilson | 11 | 0 | 1 | 0 | 0 | .091 |
| Javier | 14 | 0 | 1 | 0 | 1 | .071 |
| Ibanez | 9 | 0 | 0 | 0 | 0 | .000 |
| TOTALS | 191 | 18 | 41 | 5 | 18 | .215 |

| PITCHING | G | IP | H | BB | SO | ERA |
|---|---|---|---|---|---|---|
| Sasaki | 2 | 2⅔ | 3 | 1 | 3 | 0.00 |
| Ramsay | 2 | 1¾ | 2 | 0 | 1 | 0.00 |
| Garcia | 2 | 11⅔ | 10 | 4 | 11 | 1.54 |
| Halama | 2 | 9⅓ | 10 | 5 | 3 | 2.89 |
| Paniagua | 5 | 4⅓ | 4 | 1 | 4 | 4.15 |
| Abbott | 1 | 5 | 3 | 3 | 3 | 5.40 |
| Sele | 1 | 6 | 9 | 0 | 4 | 6.00 |
| Tomko | 2 | 5 | 3 | 4 | 4 | 7.20 |
| Mesa | 3 | 4⅓ | 5 | 3 | 3 | 12.46 |
| Rhodes | 4 | 2 | 8 | 3 | 3 | 31.50 |
| TOTALS | 6 | 52 | 57 | 25 | 41 | 5.37 |

## NATIONAL LEAGUE CHAMPIONSHIP SERIES COMPOSITE BOX SCORE

### NEW YORK METS

| BATTING | AB | R | H | HR | RBI | Avg |
|---|---|---|---|---|---|---|
| Alfonzo | 18 | 5 | 8 | 0 | 4 | .444 |
| Piazza | 17 | 7 | 7 | 2 | 4 | .412 |
| Zeile | 19 | 7 | 7 | 1 | 8 | .368 |
| Agbayani | 17 | 0 | 6 | 0 | 3 | .353 |
| Perez | 23 | 8 | 7 | 0 | 0 | .304 |
| Ventura | 14 | 4 | 3 | 0 | 5 | .214 |
| Hampton | 6 | 1 | 1 | 0 | 0 | .167 |
| Payton | 19 | 1 | 3 | 1 | 3 | .158 |
| Bordick | 13 | 2 | 1 | 0 | 0 | .077 |
| Trammell | 3 | 0 | 0 | 0 | 0 | .000 |
| Abbott | 3 | 0 | 0 | 0 | 0 | .000 |
| M. Franco | 3 | 0 | 0 | 0 | 0 | .000 |
| Hamilton | 2 | 0 | 0 | 0 | 0 | .000 |
| McEwing | 0 | 2 | 0 | 0 | 0 | .000 |
| TOTALS | 164 | 31 | 43 | 4 | 27 | .262 |

| PITCHING | G | IP | H | BB | SO | ERA |
|---|---|---|---|---|---|---|
| Hampton | 2 | 16 | 9 | 4 | 12 | 0.00 |
| Rusch | 2 | 3⅔ | 3 | 0 | 3 | 0.00 |
| Benitez | 3 | 3 | 3 | 2 | 2 | 0.00 |
| Wendell | 2 | 1⅓ | 1 | 1 | 2 | 0.00 |
| Cook | 1 | 1 | 1 | 0 | 2 | 0.00 |
| Leiter | 1 | 7 | 8 | 0 | 9 | 3.86 |
| J. Franco | 3 | 2⅔ | 3 | 2 | 2 | 6.75 |
| White | 1 | 3 | 5 | 1 | 1 | 9.00 |
| Reed | 1 | 3⅓ | 8 | 1 | 4 | 10.80 |
| B.J. Jones | 1 | 4 | 6 | 0 | 2 | 13.50 |
| TOTALS | 5 | 45 | 47 | 11 | 39 | 3.60 |

### ST. LOUIS CARDINALS

| BATTING | AB | R | H | HR | RBI | Avg |
|---|---|---|---|---|---|---|
| Hentgen | 1 | 0 | 1 | 0 | 0 | 1.000 |
| Clark | 17 | 3 | 7 | 1 | 1 | .412 |
| Drew | 12 | 2 | 4 | 0 | 1 | .333 |
| Lankford | 12 | 1 | 4 | 0 | 1 | .333 |
| Dunston | 6 | 1 | 2 | 0 | 0 | .333 |
| Benes | 3 | 1 | 1 | 0 | 0 | .333 |
| Renteria | 20 | 4 | 6 | 0 | 4 | .300 |
| Vina | 23 | 3 | 6 | 0 | 1 | .261 |
| Hernandez | 16 | 3 | 4 | 0 | 1 | .250 |
| Tatis | 13 | 1 | 3 | 0 | 2 | .231 |
| Edmonds | 22 | 1 | 5 | 1 | 5 | .227 |
| Davis | 10 | 1 | 2 | 0 | 1 | .200 |
| Polanco | 5 | 0 | 1 | 0 | 0 | .200 |
| Marrero | 4 | 0 | 0 | 0 | 0 | .000 |
| TOTALS | 177 | 21 | 47 | 2 | 18 | .266 |

| PITCHING | G | IP | H | BB | SO | ERA |
|---|---|---|---|---|---|---|
| Timlin | 3 | 3⅓ | 1 | 2 | 0 | 0.00 |
| Christiansen | 2 | 2 | 0 | 0 | 1 | 0.00 |
| Veres | 3 | 2⅓ | 2 | 0 | 3 | 0.00 |
| Reames | 2 | 6⅓ | 5 | 4 | 6 | 1.42 |
| Benes | 1 | 8 | 6 | 3 | 5 | 2.25 |
| Morris | 2 | 3⅔ | 3 | 2 | 2 | 4.91 |
| Kile | 2 | 10 | 13 | 5 | 3 | 9.00 |
| Hentgen | 1 | 3⅔ | 7 | 5 | 2 | 14.73 |
| James | 4 | 2⅓ | 5 | 1 | 0 | 15.43 |
| Ankiel | 2 | 1⅓ | 1 | 5 | 2 | 20.25 |
| TOTALS | 5 | 43 | 43 | 27 | 24 | 5.86 |

## WORLD SERIES COMPOSITE BOX SCORE

### NEW YORK YANKEES

| BATTING | AB | R | H | HR | RBI | Avg |
|---|---|---|---|---|---|---|
| Polonia | 2 | 0 | 1 | 0 | 0 | .500 |
| O'Neill | 19 | 2 | 9 | 0 | 2 | .474 |
| Jeter | 22 | 6 | 9 | 2 | 2 | .409 |
| Martinez | 22 | 3 | 8 | 0 | 2 | .364 |
| Brosius | 13 | 2 | 4 | 1 | 3 | .308 |
| Sojo | 7 | 0 | 2 | 0 | 2 | .286 |
| Vizcaino | 17 | 0 | 4 | 0 | 1 | .235 |
| Posada | 18 | 2 | 4 | 0 | 1 | .222 |
| Justice | 19 | 1 | 3 | 0 | 3 | .158 |
| Williams | 18 | 2 | 2 | 1 | 1 | .111 |
| Knoblauch | 10 | 1 | 1 | 0 | 1 | .100 |
| Hill | 3 | 0 | 0 | 0 | 0 | .000 |
| Canseco | 1 | 0 | 0 | 0 | 0 | .000 |
| Bellinger | 0 | 0 | 0 | 0 | 0 | — |
| TOTALS | 179 | 19 | 47 | 4 | 18 | .263 |

| PITCHING | G | IP | H | BB | SO | ERA |
|---|---|---|---|---|---|---|
| Clemens | 1 | 8 | 2 | 0 | 9 | 0.00 |
| Stanton | 4 | 4⅓ | 0 | 0 | 7 | 0.00 |
| Cone | 1 | 0 | 0 | 0 | 0 | 0.00 |
| Pettitte | 2 | 13⅔ | 16 | 4 | 9 | 1.98 |
| Rivera | 4 | 6 | 4 | 1 | 7 | 3.00 |
| Neagle | 1 | 4⅔ | 4 | 2 | 3 | 3.86 |
| Hernandez | 1 | 7⅓ | 9 | 3 | 12 | 4.91 |
| Nelson | 3 | 2⅔ | 5 | 1 | 1 | 10.13 |
| TOTALS | 5 | 47 | 40 | 11 | 48 | 2.68 |

### NEW YORK METS

| BATTING | AB | R | H | HR | RBI | Avg |
|---|---|---|---|---|---|---|
| Zeile | 20 | 1 | 8 | 0 | 1 | .400 |
| Trammell | 5 | 1 | 2 | 0 | 3 | .400 |
| Payton | 21 | 3 | 7 | 1 | 3 | .333 |
| Agbayani | 18 | 2 | 5 | 0 | 2 | .278 |
| Piazza | 22 | 3 | 6 | 2 | 4 | .273 |
| Abbott | 8 | 0 | 2 | 0 | 0 | .250 |
| Ventura | 20 | 1 | 3 | 1 | 1 | .150 |
| Alfonzo | 21 | 1 | 3 | 0 | 1 | .143 |
| Perez | 16 | 1 | 2 | 0 | 0 | .125 |
| Bordick | 8 | 0 | 1 | 0 | 0 | .125 |
| Hamilton | 3 | 0 | 0 | 0 | 0 | .000 |
| Harris | 4 | 1 | 0 | 0 | 0 | .000 |
| Pratt | 2 | 1 | 0 | 0 | 0 | .000 |
| McEwing | 1 | 1 | 0 | 0 | 0 | .000 |
| M. Franco | 1 | 0 | 0 | 0 | 0 | .000 |
| TOTALS | 175 | 16 | 40 | 4 | 15 | .229 |

| PITCHING | G | IP | H | BB | SO | ERA |
|---|---|---|---|---|---|---|
| J. Franco | 4 | 3⅓ | 3 | 0 | 1 | 0.00 |
| Cook | 3 | ⅔ | 1 | 3 | 1 | 0.00 |
| Rusch | 3 | 4 | 6 | 2 | 2 | 2.25 |
| Leiter | 2 | 15⅔ | 12 | 6 | 16 | 2.87 |
| Reed | 1 | 6 | 6 | 1 | 8 | 3.00 |
| Benitez | 3 | 3 | 3 | 2 | 2 | 3.00 |
| B.J. Jones | 1 | 5 | 4 | 3 | 3 | 5.40 |
| Wendell | 2 | 1⅔ | 3 | 2 | 2 | 5.40 |
| Hampton | 1 | 6 | 8 | 5 | 4 | 6.00 |
| White | 1 | 1⅓ | 1 | 1 | 1 | 6.75 |
| TOTALS | 5 | 46⅔ | 47 | 25 | 40 | 3.47 |

## WORLD SERIES INDIVIDUAL BOX SCORES

# Game 1

| NY METS | AB | R | H | RBI | BB | SO | LOB | AVG |
|---|---|---|---|---|---|---|---|---|
| Perez rf | 6 | 0 | 1 | 0 | 0 | 1 | 3 | .167 |
| Alfonzo 2b | 6 | 0 | 1 | 1 | 0 | 2 | 4 | .167 |
| Piazza dh | 5 | 0 | 1 | 0 | 0 | 1 | 3 | .200 |
| Zeile 1b | 5 | 0 | 2 | 0 | 0 | 1 | 0 | .400 |
| Ventura 3b | 5 | 0 | 0 | 0 | 1 | 1 | 4 | .000 |
| Agbayani lf | 4 | 1 | 2 | 0 | 0 | 1 | 1 | .500 |
| McEwing lf | 1 | 0 | 0 | 0 | 0 | 0 | 0 | .000 |
| Payton cf | 5 | 1 | 1 | 0 | 0 | 2 | 2 | .200 |
| Pratt c | 2 | 1 | 0 | 0 | 1 | 2 | 1 | .000 |
| Bordick ss | 1 | 0 | 0 | 0 | 0 | 1 | 1 | .000 |
| a-Trammell ph | 1 | 0 | 1 | 2 | 0 | 0 | 0 | 1.000 |
| Abbott ss | 2 | 0 | 1 | 0 | 0 | 0 | 0 | .500 |
| TOTALS | 43 | 3 | 10 | 3 | 1 | 10 | 16 | |

a—singled for Bordick in the 7th.

| NY YANKEES | AB | R | H | RBI | BB | SO | LOB | AVG |
|---|---|---|---|---|---|---|---|---|
| Knoblauch dh | 4 | 1 | 0 | 1 | 1 | 1 | 5 | .000 |
| Jeter ss | 4 | 1 | 1 | 0 | 2 | 2 | 2 | .250 |
| Justice lf | 4 | 0 | 1 | 2 | 1 | 0 | 1 | .250 |
| Bellinger pr-lf | 0 | 0 | 0 | 0 | 0 | 0 | 0 | .000 |
| b-Hill ph-lf | 1 | 0 | 0 | 0 | 0 | 0 | 2 | .000 |
| Williams cf | 4 | 0 | 0 | 0 | 2 | 1 | 1 | .000 |
| Martinez 1b | 6 | 1 | 2 | 0 | 0 | 1 | 3 | .333 |
| Posada c | 5 | 0 | 1 | 0 | 1 | 1 | 3 | .200 |
| O'Neill rf | 4 | 1 | 1 | 0 | 2 | 1 | 3 | .250 |
| Brosius 3b | 3 | 0 | 1 | 0 | 0 | 2 | 0 | .333 |
| a-Polonia ph | 1 | 1 | 1 | 0 | 0 | 0 | 0 | 1.000 |
| Sojo 3b | 2 | 0 | 0 | 0 | 0 | 0 | 3 | .000 |
| Vizcaino 2b | 6 | 0 | 4 | 1 | 0 | 1 | 0 | .667 |
| TOTALS | 44 | 4 | 12 | 4 | 9 | 8 | 25 | |

a—singled for Brosius in the 9th; b—flied to right for Bellinger in the 11th.

| | | | | | | | | | | | |
|---|---|---|---|---|---|---|---|---|---|---|---|
| NY Mets | 000 | 000 | 300 | 000— | 3 | 10 | 0 |
| NY Yankees | 000 | 002 | 001 | 001— | 4 | 12 | 0 |

LOB—Mets 8, Yankees 15. 2B—Mets: Agbayani (1), Zeile (1), Abbott (1); Yankees: Justice (1), Posada (1). Sac—Mets: Bordick (bunt); Yankees: Knoblauch (fly). CS—Mets: Piazza (1); Yankees: Knoblauch (1). GIDP—Yankees: O'Neill.

| NY METS | IP | H | R | ER | BB | SO | HR | ERA |
|---|---|---|---|---|---|---|---|---|
| Leiter | 7 | 5 | 2 | 2 | 3 | 7 | 0 | 2.57 |
| J. Franco (H, 1) | 1 | 1 | 0 | 0 | 0 | 0 | 0 | 0.00 |
| Benitez (BS, 1) | 1 | 2 | 1 | 1 | 1 | 1 | 0 | 9.00 |
| Cook | 0 | 0 | 0 | 0 | 2 | 0 | 0 | 0.00 |
| Rusch | 1⅔ | 1 | 0 | 0 | 0 | 0 | 0 | 0.00 |
| Wendell (L, 0–1) | 1 | 3 | 1 | 1 | 1 | 0 | 0 | 9.00 |

| NY YANKEES | IP | H | R | ER | BB | SO | HR | ERA |
|---|---|---|---|---|---|---|---|---|
| Pettitte | 6⅓ | 8 | 3 | 3 | 1 | 4 | 0 | 4.05 |
| Nelson | 1⅓ | 1 | 0 | 0 | 0 | 0 | 0 | 0.00 |
| Rivera | 2 | 1 | 0 | 0 | 0 | 3 | 0 | 0.00 |
| Stanton (W, 1–0) | 2 | 0 | 0 | 0 | 0 | 3 | 0 | 0.00 |

Cook pitched to 2 batters in the 10th.
WP—Rusch. IBB—Williams (by Leiter); Posada (by Rusch); O'Neill (by Wendell). HBP—Pratt (by Pettitte, by Rivera).

T—4:51. A—55,913.

## Game 2

| NY METS | AB | R | H | RBI | BB | SO | LOB | AVG |
|---|---|---|---|---|---|---|---|---|
| Perez rf | 4 | 0 | 0 | 0 | 0 | 1 | 0 | .100 |
| Alfonzo 2b | 3 | 1 | 1 | 0 | 0 | 1 | 1 | .222 |
| Piazza c | 4 | 1 | 1 | 2 | 0 | 0 | 2 | .222 |
| Ventura 3b | 4 | 0 | 1 | 0 | 0 | 1 | 1 | .111 |
| Zeile 1b | 4 | 0 | 2 | 0 | 0 | 0 | 2 | .444 |
| Agbayani lf | 4 | 1 | 1 | 0 | 0 | 2 | 2 | .375 |
| Harris dh | 4 | 1 | 0 | 0 | 0 | 1 | 2 | .000 |
| Payton cf | 4 | 1 | 1 | 3 | 0 | 1 | 0 | .222 |
| Bordick ss | 2 | 0 | 0 | 0 | 0 | 1 | 0 | .000 |
| a-Hamilton ph | 1 | 0 | 0 | 0 | 0 | 1 | 0 | .000 |
| Abbott ss | 1 | 0 | 0 | 0 | 0 | 1 | 0 | .333 |
| TOTALS | 35 | 5 | 7 | 5 | 0 | 10 | 10 | |

a—struck out for Bordick in the 8th.

| NY YANKEES | AB | R | H | RBI | BB | SO | LOB | AVG |
|---|---|---|---|---|---|---|---|---|
| Knoblauch dh | 4 | 0 | 0 | 0 | 1 | 0 | 0 | .000 |
| Jeter ss | 5 | 1 | 3 | 0 | 0 | 1 | 0 | .444 |
| Justice lf | 3 | 1 | 0 | 0 | 1 | 1 | 2 | .143 |
| Bellinger lf | 0 | 0 | 0 | 0 | 0 | 0 | 0 | .000 |
| Williams cf | 3 | 1 | 0 | 0 | 2 | 0 | 2 | .000 |
| Martinez 1b | 5 | 1 | 3 | 2 | 0 | 0 | 0 | .455 |
| Posada c | 3 | 1 | 2 | 1 | 2 | 0 | 2 | .375 |
| O'Neill rf | 4 | 0 | 3 | 1 | 0 | 1 | 2 | .500 |
| Brosius 3b | 3 | 1 | 1 | 2 | 0 | 1 | 4 | .333 |
| Vizcaino 2b | 4 | 0 | 0 | 0 | 0 | 1 | 1 | .400 |
| TOTALS | 34 | 6 | 12 | 6 | 6 | 5 | 13 | |

| | | | | | |
|---|---|---|---|---|---|
| NY Mets | 0 0 0 | 0 0 0 | 0 0 5 | —5 7 3 |
| NY Yankees | 2 1 0 | 0 1 0 | 1 1 x | —6 12 1 |

E—Mets: Payton (1), Bordick (1), Perez (1); Yankees: Clemens (1). LOB—Mets 4, Yankees 12. 2B—Yankees: Martinez (1), Jeter 2 (2), O'Neill (1). HR—Mets: Piazza (1), Payton (1); Yankees: Brosius (1). CS—Yankees: Vizcaino (1). Sac—Yankees: Brosius (fly).

| NY METS | IP | H | R | ER | BB | SO | HR | ERA |
|---|---|---|---|---|---|---|---|---|
| Hampton (L, 0–1) | 6 | 8 | 4 | 4 | 5 | 4 | 1 | 6.00 |
| Rusch | ⅓ | 2 | 1 | 1 | 0 | 0 | 0 | 4.50 |
| White | 1⅓ | 1 | 1 | 1 | 1 | 1 | 0 | 6.75 |
| Cook | ⅓ | 1 | 0 | 0 | 0 | 0 | 0 | 0.00 |

| NY YANKEES | IP | H | R | ER | BB | SO | HR | ERA |
|---|---|---|---|---|---|---|---|---|
| Clemens (W, 1–0) | 8 | 2 | 0 | 0 | 0 | 9 | 0 | 0.00 |
| Nelson | 0 | 3 | 3 | 3 | 0 | 0 | 1 | 20.25 |
| Rivera | 1 | 2 | 2 | 2 | 0 | 1 | 1 | 6.00 |

Nelson pitched to 3 batters in the 9th.
WP—Clemens. IBB—Posada (by Hampton), Williams (by White). HBP—Alfonzo (by Clemens); Justice (by Hampton).

T—3:30. A—56,059.

## Game 3

| NY YANKEES | AB | R | H | RBI | BB | SO | LOB | AVG |
|---|---|---|---|---|---|---|---|---|
| Vizcaino 2b | 4 | 0 | 0 | 0 | 0 | 2 | 2 | .286 |
| c-Polonia ph | 1 | 0 | 0 | 0 | 0 | 0 | 1 | .500 |
| Jeter ss | 4 | 1 | 2 | 0 | 1 | 2 | 1 | .462 |
| Justice lf | 3 | 0 | 1 | 1 | 1 | 0 | 2 | .200 |
| Williams cf | 4 | 0 | 0 | 0 | 0 | 2 | 4 | .000 |
| Martinez 1b | 3 | 1 | 1 | 0 | 1 | 1 | 1 | .429 |
| Posada c | 4 | 0 | 0 | 0 | 0 | 2 | 2 | .250 |
| O'Neill rf | 4 | 0 | 3 | 1 | 0 | 0 | 0 | .583 |
| Brosius 3b | 2 | 0 | 0 | 0 | 0 | 1 | 1 | .250 |
| a-Hill ph | 1 | 0 | 0 | 0 | 0 | 0 | 1 | .000 |
| Sojo 3b | 0 | 0 | 0 | 0 | 0 | 0 | 0 | .000 |
| Hernandez p | 2 | 0 | 0 | 0 | 0 | 2 | 1 | .000 |
| Stanton p | 0 | 0 | 0 | 0 | 0 | 0 | 0 | .000 |
| b-Knoblauch ph | 1 | 0 | 1 | 0 | 0 | 0 | 0 | .111 |
| TOTALS | 33 | 2 | 8 | 2 | 3 | 12 | 16 | |

a—flied to right for Brosius in the 8th; b—singled for Stanton in the 9th; c—flied to center for Vizcaino in the 9th.

| NY METS | AB | R | H | RBI | BB | SO | LOB | AVG |
|---|---|---|---|---|---|---|---|---|
| Perez rf | 3 | 0 | 0 | 0 | 1 | 1 | 1 | .077 |
| Alfonzo 2b | 4 | 0 | 0 | 0 | 0 | 2 | 3 | .154 |
| Piazza c | 4 | 1 | 1 | 0 | 0 | 2 | 0 | .231 |
| Ventura 3b | 3 | 1 | 2 | 1 | 1 | 1 | 0 | .250 |
| Zeile 1b | 4 | 1 | 2 | 1 | 0 | 2 | 1 | .462 |
| Agbayani lf | 3 | 0 | 1 | 1 | 1 | 1 | 1 | .364 |
| McEwing pr-lf | 0 | 1 | 0 | 0 | 0 | 0 | 0 | .000 |
| Payton cf | 4 | 0 | 1 | 0 | 0 | 2 | 3 | .231 |
| Bordick ss | 3 | 0 | 1 | 0 | 0 | 1 | 3 | .167 |
| b-Harris ph | 0 | 0 | 0 | 0 | 0 | 0 | 0 | .000 |
| c-Trammell ph | 0 | 0 | 0 | 1 | 0 | 0 | 1 | 1.000 |
| Reed p | 1 | 0 | 1 | 0 | 0 | 0 | 0 | 1.000 |
| a-Hamilton ph | 1 | 0 | 0 | 0 | 0 | 0 | 3 | .000 |
| d-Abbott ph-ss | 1 | 0 | 0 | 0 | 0 | 1 | 1 | .250 |
| TOTALS | 31 | 4 | 9 | 4 | 3 | 13 | 17 | |

a—hit into fielder's choice for Reed in the 6th; b—pinch-hit for Bordick in the 8th; c—hit sacrifice fly for Harris in the 8th; d—struck out for J. Franco in the 8th.

| | | | | |
|---|---|---|---|---|
| Yankees | 0 0 1 | 1 0 0 | 0 0 0 | —2 8 0 |
| Mets | 0 1 0 | 0 0 1 | 0 2 x | —4 9 0 |

LOB—Yankees 10, Mets 8. 2B—Yankees: O'Neill (2), Justice (2); Mets: Ventura (1), Piazza (1), Zeile (2), Agbayani (2). 3B—Yankees: O'Neill (1). HR—Mets: Ventura (1). Sac—Yankees: O. Hernandez (bunt); Mets: Reed (bunt), Trammell (fly). GIDP—Yankees: Posada.

| NY YANKEES | IP | H | R | ER | BB | SO | HR | ERA |
|---|---|---|---|---|---|---|---|---|
| Hernandez (L, 0–1) | 7⅓ | 9 | 4 | 4 | 3 | 12 | 1 | 4.91 |
| Stanton | ⅔ | 0 | 0 | 0 | 0 | 1 | 0 | 0.00 |

| NY METS | IP | H | R | ER | BB | SO | HR | ERA |
|---|---|---|---|---|---|---|---|---|
| Reed | 6 | 6 | 2 | 2 | 1 | 8 | 0 | 3.00 |
| Wendell | ⅔ | 0 | 0 | 0 | 1 | 2 | 0 | 5.40 |
| Cook | ⅓ | 0 | 0 | 0 | 1 | 1 | 0 | 0.00 |
| J. Franco (W, 1–0) | 1 | 1 | 0 | 0 | 0 | 0 | 0 | 0.00 |
| Benitez (S,1) | 1 | 1 | 0 | 0 | 0 | 1 | 0 | 4.50 |

Cook pitched to 1 batter in the 8th.
HBP—Brosius (by Reed).

T—3:39. A—55,299.

## Game 4

| NY YANKEES | AB | R | H | RBI | BB | SO | LOB | AVG |
|---|---|---|---|---|---|---|---|---|
| Jeter ss | 5 | 2 | 2 | 1 | 0 | 1 | 1 | .444 |
| Sojo 2b | 4 | 0 | 1 | 1 | 1 | 0 | 0 | .167 |
| Justice lf | 5 | 0 | 0 | 0 | 0 | 0 | 3 | .133 |
| Bellinger lf | 0 | 0 | 0 | 0 | 0 | 0 | 0 | .000 |
| Williams cf | 4 | 0 | 0 | 0 | 0 | 1 | 2 | .000 |
| Martinez 1b | 4 | 0 | 2 | 0 | 0 | 1 | 0 | .444 |
| O'Neill rf | 4 | 1 | 2 | 0 | 0 | 0 | 2 | .563 |
| Posada c | 3 | 0 | 0 | 0 | 1 | 1 | 1 | .200 |
| Brosius 3b | 1 | 0 | 1 | 1 | 2 | 0 | 1 | .333 |
| Neagle p | 2 | 0 | 0 | 0 | 0 | 1 | 3 | .000 |
| a-Canseco ph | 1 | 0 | 0 | 0 | 0 | 1 | 2 | .000 |
| Rivera p | 1 | 0 | 0 | 0 | 0 | 0 | 1 | .000 |
| TOTALS | 34 | 3 | 8 | 3 | 4 | 6 | 16 | |

a—struck out for Cone in the 6th.

| NY METS | AB | R | H | RBI | BB | SO | LOB | AVG |
|---|---|---|---|---|---|---|---|---|
| Perez rf | 3 | 1 | 1 | 0 | 0 | 1 | 0 | .125 |
| d-Abbott ph-ss | 1 | 0 | 0 | 0 | 0 | 1 | 1 | .200 |
| Alfonzo 2b | 3 | 0 | 0 | 0 | 1 | 0 | 0 | .125 |
| Piazza c | 4 | 1 | 1 | 2 | 0 | 1 | 1 | .235 |
| Zeile 1b | 4 | 0 | 2 | 0 | 0 | 0 | 1 | .471 |
| McEwing pr | 0 | 0 | 0 | 0 | 0 | 0 | 0 | .000 |
| Benitez p | 0 | 0 | 0 | 0 | 0 | 0 | 0 | .000 |
| Ventura 3b | 4 | 0 | 0 | 0 | 0 | 0 | 2 | .188 |
| Agbayani lf | 3 | 0 | 0 | 0 | 1 | 1 | 1 | .286 |
| Payton cf | 4 | 0 | 2 | 0 | 0 | 1 | 0 | .294 |
| Bordick ss | 2 | 0 | 0 | 0 | 0 | 0 | 3 | .125 |
| a-Harris ph | 0 | 0 | 0 | 0 | 1 | 0 | 0 | .000 |
| J. Franco p | 0 | 0 | 0 | 0 | 0 | 0 | 0 | .000 |
| M. Franco 1b | 1 | 0 | 0 | 0 | 0 | 1 | 0 | .000 |
| B.J. Jones p | 2 | 0 | 0 | 0 | 0 | 1 | 3 | .000 |
| Rusch p | 0 | 0 | 0 | 0 | 0 | 0 | 0 | .000 |
| b-Hamilton ph | 0 | 0 | 0 | 0 | 0 | 0 | 0 | .000 |
| c-Trammell ph-rf | 1 | 0 | 0 | 0 | 0 | 1 | 1 | .500 |
| TOTALS | 32 | 2 | 6 | 2 | 3 | 11 | 13 | |

a—walked for Bordick in the 7th; b—pinch-hit for Rusch in the 7th; c—struck out for Hamilton in the 7th; d—struck out for Perez in the 7th.

| | | | | |
|---|---|---|---|---|
| NY Yankees | 1 1 1 | 0 0 0 | 0 0 0 | —3 8 0 |
| NY Mets | 0 0 2 | 0 0 0 | 0 0 0 | —2 6 1 |

E—Mets: Trammell (1). LOB—Yankees: 9, Mets 6. 3B—Yankees: O'Neill (2), Jeter (1). HR—Yankees: Jeter (1); Mets: Piazza (2). SB—Yankees: Sojo (1). Sac—Yankees: Brosius (fly). GIDP—Yankees: O'Neill.

| NY YANKEES | IP | H | R | ER | BB | SO | HR | ERA |
|---|---|---|---|---|---|---|---|---|
| Neagle | 4⅔ | 4 | 2 | 2 | 2 | 3 | 1 | 3.86 |
| Cone | ⅓ | 0 | 0 | 0 | 0 | 0 | 0 | 0.00 |
| Nelson (W, 1–0) | 1⅓ | 1 | 0 | 0 | 1 | 1 | 0 | 10.12 |
| Stanton (H,1) | ⅔ | 0 | 0 | 0 | 0 | 2 | 0 | 0.00 |
| Rivera (S,1) | 2 | 1 | 0 | 0 | 0 | 2 | 0 | 3.60 |

| NY METS | IP | H | R | ER | BB | SO | HR | ERA |
|---|---|---|---|---|---|---|---|---|
| B.J. Jones (L, 0–1) | 5 | 4 | 3 | 3 | 3 | 3 | 1 | 5.40 |
| Rusch | 2 | 3 | 0 | 0 | 0 | 2 | 0 | 2.25 |
| J. Franco | 1 | 1 | 0 | 0 | 0 | 1 | 0 | 0.00 |
| Benitez | 1 | 0 | 0 | 0 | 1 | 0 | 0 | 3.00 |

IBB—Posada (by B.J. Jones); Brosius (by B.J. Jones).

T—3:20. A—55,290.

## Game 5

| NY YANKEES | AB | R | H | RBI | BB | SO | LOB | AVG |
|---|---|---|---|---|---|---|---|---|
| Vizcaino 2b | 3 | 0 | 0 | 0 | 0 | 1 | 0 | .235 |
| a-Knoblauch ph | 1 | 0 | 0 | 0 | 0 | 0 | 0 | .100 |
| Stanton p | 0 | 0 | 0 | 0 | 0 | 0 | 0 | .000 |
| b-Hill ph | 1 | 0 | 0 | 0 | 0 | 0 | 1 | .000 |
| Rivera p | 0 | 0 | 0 | 0 | 0 | 0 | 0 | .000 |
| Jeter ss | 4 | 1 | 1 | 1 | 0 | 2 | 0 | .409 |
| Justice lf | 4 | 0 | 1 | 0 | 0 | 1 | 0 | .158 |
| Bellinger lf | 0 | 0 | 0 | 0 | 0 | 0 | 0 | .000 |
| Williams cf | 3 | 1 | 2 | 1 | 1 | 1 | 1 | .111 |
| Martinez 1b | 4 | 0 | 0 | 0 | 0 | 1 | 2 | .364 |
| O'Neill rf | 3 | 0 | 0 | 0 | 1 | 2 | 0 | .474 |
| Posada c | 3 | 1 | 1 | 0 | 1 | 0 | 1 | .222 |
| Brosius 3b | 4 | 1 | 1 | 0 | 0 | 0 | 1 | .308 |
| Pettitte p | 3 | 0 | 0 | 0 | 0 | 1 | 2 | .000 |
| Sojo 2b | 1 | 0 | 1 | 1 | 0 | 0 | 0 | .286 |
| TOTALS | 34 | 4 | 7 | 3 | 3 | 9 | 8 | |

a—fouled to catcher for Vizcaino in the 8th; b—flied to left for Stanton in the 9th.

| NY METS | AB | R | H | RBI | BB | SO | LOB | AVG |
|---|---|---|---|---|---|---|---|---|
| Agbayani lf | 4 | 0 | 1 | 1 | 1 | 1 | 2 | .278 |
| Alfonzo 2b | 5 | 0 | 1 | 0 | 0 | 0 | 2 | .143 |
| Piazza c | 5 | 0 | 2 | 0 | 0 | 0 | 2 | .273 |
| Zeile 1b | 3 | 0 | 0 | 0 | 1 | 2 | 2 | .400 |
| Ventura 3b | 4 | 0 | 0 | 0 | 0 | 2 | 3 | .150 |
| Trammell rf | 3 | 1 | 1 | 0 | 1 | 0 | 0 | .400 |
| Perez rf | 0 | 0 | 0 | 0 | 0 | 0 | 0 | .125 |
| Payton cf | 4 | 1 | 2 | 0 | 0 | 1 | 1 | .333 |
| Abbott ss | 3 | 0 | 1 | 0 | 1 | 0 | 0 | .250 |
| Leiter p | 2 | 0 | 0 | 0 | 0 | 0 | 3 | .000 |
| J. Franco p | 0 | 0 | 0 | 0 | 0 | 0 | 0 | .000 |
| a-Hamilton ph | 1 | 0 | 0 | 0 | 0 | 1 | 0 | .000 |

a—struck out for J. Franco in the 9th.

| | | | | |
|---|---|---|---|---|
| NY Yankees | 0 1 0 | 0 0 1 | 0 0 2 | —4 7 1 |
| NY Mets | 0 2 0 | 0 0 0 | 0 0 0 | —2 8 1 |

E—Yankees: Pettitte (1); Mets: Payton (2). LOB—Yankees 6, Mets 10. 2B—Mets: Piazza (2). HR—Yankees: Williams (1), Jeter (2). PO—Mets: Abbott (1). Sac—Mets: Leiter (bunt).

| NY YANKEES | IP | H | R | ER | BB | SO | HR | ERA |
|---|---|---|---|---|---|---|---|---|
| Pettitte | 7 | 8 | 2 | 0 | 3 | 5 | 0 | 1.98 |
| Stanton (W, 2–0) | 1 | 0 | 0 | 0 | 0 | 1 | 0 | 0.00 |
| Rivera (S, 2) | 1 | 0 | 0 | 0 | 1 | 1 | 0 | 3.00 |

| NY METS | IP | H | R | ER | BB | SO | HR | ERA |
|---|---|---|---|---|---|---|---|---|
| Leiter (L, 0–1) | 8⅔ | 7 | 4 | 3 | 3 | 9 | 2 | 2.87 |
| J. Franco | ⅓ | 0 | 0 | 0 | 0 | 0 | 0 | 0.00 |

IBB—Zeile (by Pettitte).

T—3:32. A—55,292.

# Photo Credits

Cover: Chang W. Lee
Back cover: Chang W. Lee

Front Matter
Half-title page, Ozier Muhammad; Title page, Ozier Muhammad.

Introduction
7, The New York Times; 8, both, National Baseball Hall of Fame Library, Cooperstown, N.Y.; 9, Corbis; 10, Corbis; 11, Mark Kauffman.

The Regular Season
12-13, Vincent Laforet; 14, Chang W. Lee; 15, Chang W. Lee; 16, Barton Silverman; 17, both, G. Paul Burnett; 18, Vincent Laforet; 19, Barton Silverman; 20, Vincent Laforet; 21, Vincent Laforet; 22-23, Barton Silverman; 24, G. Paul Burnett; 25, G. Paul Burnett; 26, G. Paul Burnett; 27, left, Ozier Muhammad; right, G. Paul Burnett; 28, G. Paul Burnett; 29, Ozier Muhammad; 30, both, Ozier Muhammad; 31, G. Paul Burnett; 32, G. Paul Burnett; 33, G. Paul Burnett; 34, G. Paul Burnett; 35, Ozier Muhammad; 36, G. Paul Burnett; 37, Ozier Muhammad; 38, both, G. Paul Burnett; 39, G. Paul Burnett; 40, Ozier Muhammad; 41, Ozier Muhammad; 42, G. Paul Burnett; 43, Chang W. Lee; 44, left, Ozier Muhammad; center, Chang W. Lee; 45, Ozier Muhammad; 46, G. Paul Burnett; 47, Chang W. Lee; 48, Chang W. Lee; 49, both, Ozier Muhammad; 50, Chang W. Lee; 51, Chang W. Lee.

The Playoffs
52, Barton Silverman; 53, Vincent Laforet; 54, Barton Silverman; 55, left, Barton Silverman; right, Chang W. Lee; 56, Vincent Laforet; 57, Vincent Laforet; 58, both, Vincent Laforet; 59, Chang W. Lee; 60, Chang W. Lee; 61, Barton Silverman; 62, left, Vincent Laforet; center, Chang W. Lee; 63, Chang W. Lee; 64, Barton Silverman; 65, left, Vincent Laforet; right, Barton Silverman; 66, Vincent Laforet; 67, Chang W. Lee; 68, Barton Silverman; 69, Barton Silverman; 70, both, Vincent Laforet; 71, Mike Blake/Reuters; 72, Barton Silverman; 73, Barton Silverman; 74, Barton Silverman; 75, Vincent Laforet; 76-77, both, Vincent Laforet; 78, left, Barton Silverman; right, Vincent Laforet; 79, Vincent Laforet; 80, Chang W. Lee; 81, Vincent Laforet; 82, Vincent Laforet; 83, Vincent Laforet.

The World Series
84-85, Chang W. Lee; 86, G. Paul Burnett; 87, Barton Silverman; 88, Vincent Laforet; 89, top, Ruby Washington; bottom, Vincent Laforet; 90, Barton Silverman; 91, Barton Silverman; 92, Ozier Muhammad; 93, Vincent Laforet; 94, Barton Silverman; 95, top, G. Paul Burnett; bottom, Barton Silverman; 96, Chang W. Lee; 97, Barton Silverman; 98, left, Chang W. Lee; center, Vincent Laforet; 99, G. Paul Burnett; 100, G. Paul Burnett; 101, Barton Silverman; 102, Chang W. Lee; 103, Chang W. Lee; 104, Vincent Laforet; 105, Chang W. Lee; 106, both, Chang W. Lee; 107,.Vincent Laforet; 108, Vincent Laforet; 109, Chang W. Lee; 110, Chang W. Lee; 111, Barton Silverman; 112, Ozier Muhammad; 113, top, Chang W. Lee; bottom, Barton Silverman; 114.

True Believers: The Fans
120, Ozier Muhammad; 121, top left, Chang W. Lee; top right, G. Paul Burnett; bottom left, G. Paul Burnett; bottom right, Chang W. Lee; 122, top, Ozier Muhammad; bottom left, G. Paul Burnett; bottom right, Barton Silverman; 123, top, Chang W. Lee; bottom, Barton Silverman.